OCT -- 2017

BAKED

Adelle Smith
Photography by Daniel Annett

BAKED

AMAZING BAKES TO CREATE WITH YOUR CHILD

ORCHARD

ORCHARD BOOKS

First published in Great Britain in 2016 by The Watts Publishing Group

1 3 5 7 9 10 8 6 4 2

Text © Adelle Smith, 2016

Illustrations © BKD London LTD

Photography by Daniel Annett
Illustrations by Cécile Dumetier
Props and food styling by Adelle Smith

The moral rights of the author have been asserted.

All rights reserved.

A CIP catalogue record for this book is available from the British Library.

ISBN 978 1 40834 402 6

Printed and bound in Italy

Orchard Books
An imprint of Hachette Children's Group
Part of The Watts Publishing Group Limited
Carmelite House
50 Victoria Embankment
London EC4Y ODZ

An Hachette UK Company

www.hachette.co.uk

www.hachettechildrens.co.uk

CONTENTS

INTRODUCTION

"I love seeing the kids' imaginations run wild and the enjoyment they get from producing something they are really proud of."

ADELLE SMITH

I am a self-taught baker. As a child I loved baking with my nan, and now I'm always trying out new recipes and putting my own spin on them, seeing what works and what doesn't.

The kitchen is the heart of our home. My husband, Mark, is an absolute foodie and our children enjoy baking and getting creative with us. My kitchen is also where my company, BKD (aka Baked), was born, running themed baking classes for children and supplying children's creative baking kits. BKD bakes are vibrant, contemporary, unisex and – of course – super tasty.

It's so important to take time out in our busy lives to have one-on-one time with our children. Baking together gives the perfect opportunity to reconnect with your child and – if you try not to worry about the mess – it can be a great stress-buster for you. Baking at home with your family should be easy, relaxed and, above all, fun!

Baking is a great way to introduce your child to cooking, teaching them a lifelong skill and helping them feel good about food. Following recipes can help children with their reading, and measuring quantities uses their maths skills.

As your child learns, and you encourage them, it will build both their knowledge and their self-esteem. There's nothing better than seeing your child beam with pride at what they've created with you. I get such a buzz from seeing the huge sense of achievement children show when they hold up a twenty-eyed spider cookie they've made at one of our events.

The majority of the projects in this book are designed to be easy enough for mini bakers as young as three to get involved with, and the featured difficulty guide will help you decide which project to make with your child, or which to make for them for that show-stopper birthday cake.

There are recipe sections featuring a selection of my most-loved baking recipes for frostings and fillings, cupcakes, cakes and biscuits, with lots of flavour options to try. You can use these sections by themselves – if you want to whip up a simple batch of cupcakes or cookies, for example, perfect for a rainy Sunday with your family – or be bold and get into the fun BKD spirit by using the projects within each section to create eye-catching bakes: from my signature rainbow unicorn cupcakes, inspired by my stepdaughter, Elsie, to the super-stylish dino cake I created for my son, Cai.

Throughout the book are my tips and tricks to help you learn how to bake like a pro and add your own stamp to things, to produce unique and fabulous masterpieces.

Happy baking!

FOUNDER AND CREATIVE DIRECTOR

1

BASICS

Before you bake, it's important to have everything you need. In this section, you will find tips, tricks and suggestions for equipment I consider great additions to your baking toolkit, as well as my larder essentials and good-to-haves. I have also included a range of techniques to help you and your child learn the basics of baking and cake decorating.

Before even cracking open an egg, ensure you read through the project and all the recipes needed for it. Preparation is especially important when baking with young children. Things can get a little wild, and you wouldn't want to get halfway through and realise you are missing the googly eyes for the rainbow unicorn cupcakes, or the flames for your roaring rocket cake!

TOOLS

To make the recipes and projects in this book you'll need some basic tools to ensure you get amazing results. Here are the things I suggest you consider including in your baking toolkit.

Baking

electronic scales

measuring jug

electric stand mixer

electric hand mixer

spatula

sieve

mixing bowls

saucepan

wooden rolling pin

silicone spoon

measuring spoons

spoons

cup scoop

zester

baking parchment

cling film

scissors

cupcake cases

cake tester

cupcake corer

baking sheet
(with flat edges)

wire rack

cake tins (round)

cake tins (rectangular)

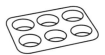

muffin tins

apron

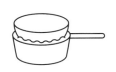

bain-marie

cookie cutters

Sugarcraft and Decorating

non-stick mats

sugar/flour shaker

craft knife

ruler

piping bags and nozzles

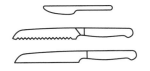

knives

silicone rolling pin

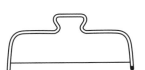

cake-cutting wire

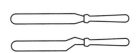

regular and offset palette knives

stainless steel scrapers

turntable

cocktail sticks

fine paintbrushes

sugarcraft modelling tools

cake-pop sticks

cake boards

For cakes, cookies, frostings and fillings

FLOUR
plain flour
self-raising flour
wholemeal flour

SUGAR
caster sugar
soft light brown sugar
icing sugar
golden syrup

RAISING AGENTS
bicarbonate of soda
baking powder

DAIRY AND EGGS
double cream
milk
full-fat cream cheese
  (Philadelphia™ gives the best results)
unsalted butter
free-range (or organic) eggs

IN MY LARDER

Always try to buy the best ingredients you can. It really does make a big difference to the taste of your bakes. Avoid cheap butters as they have a high water content, and always buy free-range or organic eggs. Keeping a few of the basics below in your cupboards at home will make impromptu baking sessions with the kids on a rainy weekend feel fuss-free!

For decorating

CHOCOLATE
chocolate chips
cooking chocolate bars
cocoa powder
candy melts

SPICES
ground ginger
ground cinnamon

FLAVOURINGS
essences
freeze-dried fruit powders
fresh fruits such as
    lemons, oranges
    and raspberries
fruit jams
sea salt flakes

ROLL-OUT ICING
coloured sugarpaste

SPRINKLES
edible silver balls
00s
sugar strands
sugar shapes

SWEETS
coloured chocolate buttons
chocolate sticks
mini marshmallows
large marshmallows
dolly mixture
jelly beans
strawberry cables
fizzy strawberry laces
edible candy eyes
Oreos™

LUSTRES AND GLITTERS
edible glitter
edible gold and silver
    lustre spray

OTHER
icing writers
edible glue
food colouring gels
non-stick cooking spray
vegetable shortening

TIPS, TRICKS AND TECHNIQUES

Each baking section begins with a selection of classic recipes, which you can use as a great basis for all the step-by-step projects in the book and, of course, your own cake decorating creations.

Enjoy the recipes and projects with your child, or surprise your family and friends with a show-stopper birthday cake!

Difficulty Guide

Most of my projects are suitable for kids as young as three to get involved with. You will know your own child's capabilities, but I have also graded projects to help you judge how much help they'll need.

Easy-peasy

Give it a go

Pretty tricky

Safety Alerts

Safety is so important when having fun in the kitchen with your kids. Hot pans and sharp knives are often involved in baking, and both are areas for caution. To alert you to these possible dangers, you will see these two warning signs used throughout the book:

WARNING Hot

WARNING Sharp Knives

Do point out the warning signs in the book and explain to your kids why safety in the kitchen is so important. Remember to always keep yourself between your kids and any hot pans and sharp knives.

Flavour Options

The recipes in this book are some of my tried-and-tested favourites. Look for this symbol to see how to adapt them for lots of different flavour options.

Ingredient Temperatures

Having ingredients at the correct temperature will greatly improve your bakes. Butter and eggs should always be used at room temperature. Butter that's too cold can be cubed and gently heated in the microwave – take care not to melt it. Cold eggs can be placed in tepid water, not hot.

Your Oven

All of the recipes in this book have been tested with a fan-assisted oven. If you have a conventional oven, increase the temperatures given by 20°C /70°F. Oven temperatures can vary greatly, so you may also want to use an oven thermometer.

Preheat your oven at least 20 minutes before you bake. And never open the oven door mid-baking. I know it's tempting!

Hygiene

Remember to roll up your sleeves, wear aprons and wash your hands before you start. It's also good practice to clear enough space in the kitchen. Working around lots of dirty pans risks cross-contamination and can cause accidents.

Sharing is Caring

Encourage your kids to share their creations, and have family members compliment them on how yummy they taste and how good they look. It's a great way to boost your children's confidence and teach them from a young age that sharing is fun!

HOW TO LINE A CAKE TIN

Lining your cake tins is so important if you want perfect-looking cakes.
I always line my tins – it's really worth the extra few minutes before you start.
Children love getting their fingers mucky greasing the tins!

Round cake tin

01   Place a piece of baking parchment on the work surface and put the cake tin on it. Draw around the cake tin. Cut out the circular base with scissors, cutting along the inside of the line you've drawn.

02   Wrap the baking parchment around the tin to measure the length you need. I cut mine slightly longer so it overlaps in the tin. Then cut so the height is about 8cm above the cake tin. Next, fold it back about 3cm along its length and make angled snips along the whole length.

03   Use a piece of baking parchment with a little butter on it to grease the inside of the cake tin. Get your kids to help with this.

04   Press the strip around the inside of the tin. Then add the circular base. Make sure the parchment is pressed firmly on to the tin – the butter will help it stick.

Rectangular or square cake tin

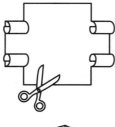

01   Measure the length and width of the cake tin. Then measure its depth, and add this, plus 5cm, to the length and width measurements. Cut a piece of baking parchment to this size.

02   Place the baking parchment on the work surface and put the cake tin in the centre. Make four cuts from the edge of the baking parchment to the corners of the tin.

03   Use a piece of baking parchment with a little butter on it to grease the inside of the cake tin. Get your kids to help with this.

04   Press the baking parchment on to the inside of the cake tin and fold and overlap it at the corners. The butter will hold it tight.

HOW TO SPLIT, FILL AND COVER CAKES IN BUTTERCREAM

I always cover my cakes with a crumb coating to seal in any loose cake crumbs and fill any holes – essential for a crisp buttercream finish.

Your finished cake will only look as good as what's underneath the buttercream, and getting a nice straight top and sides will make you look like a baking pro!

Cutting

TIP:

If using a cake cutting wire, ensure you always keep the feet touching the cutting board and use a zigzag motion to cut.

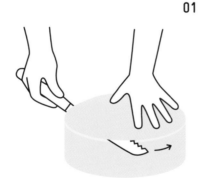

01 Place the cooled cake on a cutting board and rest the palm of your hand on top of the cake to prevent it from moving. Using a cake cutting wire or a serrated knife, cut the top dome off the cake using a gentle sawing motion.

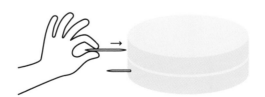

02 For a single big cake, repeat the process halfway down your cake to cut it in half. Place a cocktail stick in each half, aligned vertically. This will allow you to fill your cake and then put the two pieces back together in the same place.

Filling

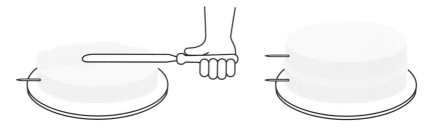

TIP:

When using two separately baked cake layers, I always tip my top layer upside down so that the cake's bottom is on top, giving a nice flat top to my cakes.

01 Attach the bottom layer of your cake to the cake board with a little buttercream (p. 32), cake-base side down.

02 Using a palette knife, spread evenly with a generous amount of buttercream filling. Don't worry about it coming out at the edges a little – if you're covering the cake in buttercream it won't matter. You just want a nice smooth finish.

03 If you wish to add a second filling, such as raspberry jam, use a clean palette knife to spread it evenly on to the buttercream filling layer. You'll need less jam than buttercream. Again, aim for a smooth finish.

04 Place the top layer on top of the bottom, lining up the cocktail sticks if you've used them.

05 Remove the cocktail sticks, if used, and smooth away any excess filling with the palette knife.

Crumb Coating

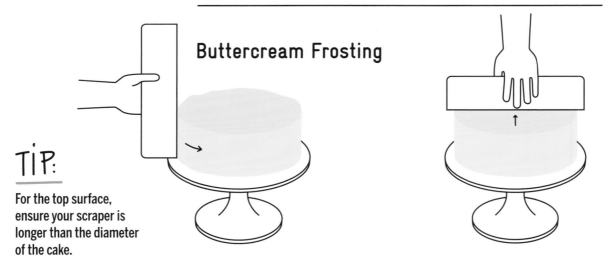

TIP:

A turntable will make
this much easier.

01 Using a palette knife or scraper, spread a thin layer of buttercream all over your cake, ensuring the whole surface is covered. Try to get an even finish where the cake sections join, and fill any small holes, so the outside is flat and smooth.

02 Put your cake in the fridge for a minimum of 60 minutes to crust over and firm up, before covering in the top coating of buttercream.

Buttercream Frosting

TIP:

For the top surface,
ensure your scraper is
longer than the diameter
of the cake.

01 Cover your cake in a generous layer of buttercream using a palette knife or an offset spatula.

02 For the sides: spin the turntable in a continuous motion while holding the scraper at a 90-degree angle, lightly touching the surface of the cake. The bottom of the scraper should be touching the cake board or turntable.

03 For the top: if you are not happy with the finish of the top of your cake, you can drag the scraper towards you across the top in a continuous motion.

Now go mad and decorate your cake however you wish!

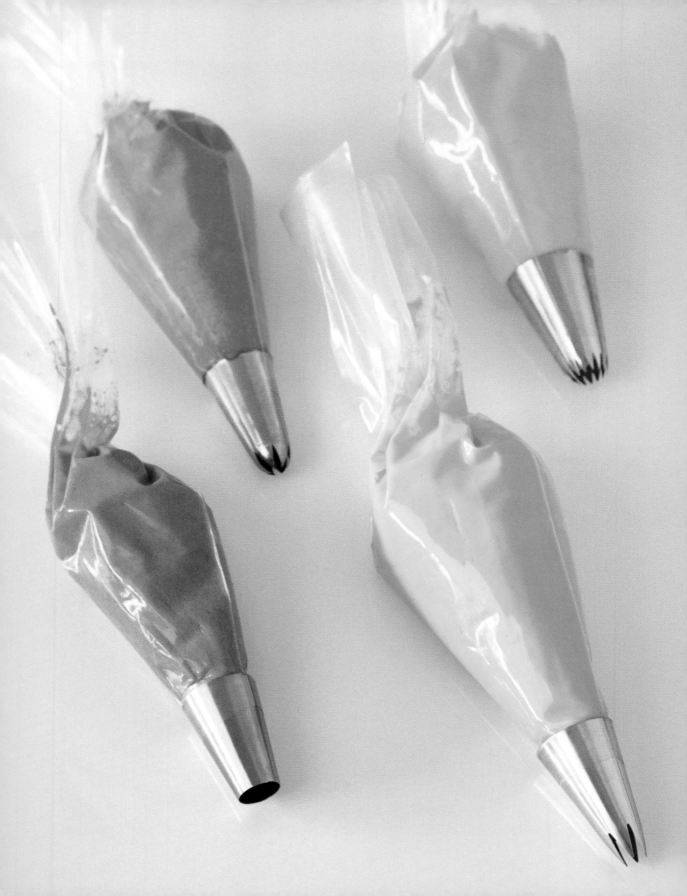

HOW TO FILL AND USE A PIPING BAG

I like to use disposable plastic piping bags, but you can also get the reusable fabric type, and mini paper piping bags are useful for royal icing. Use whichever you feel comfortable with. Piping bags are perfect for filling and frosting cupcakes, adding details to cakes and piping cookies and meringues.

TIP:

To make it easier for younger children, I give the piping bag a second twist halfway down. The adult holds the piping bag below the top twist and the child holds and squeezes just below the halfway twist with their dominant hand. This method requires less strength to push the filling out.

01

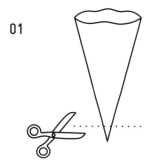

Snip the end of your piping bag and insert the nozzle. Ensure you don't cut too far up the bag – if the hole is too big, the nozzle will push out when you squeeze the bag.

02

Take the piping bag and fold over the top like a cuff. Hold it under the folded area.

03

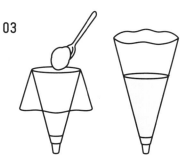

Fill the piping bag with buttercream or icing using a tablespoon or spatula. Aim to get the filling as far down the bag as possible and take care not to overfill the bag. Pull the cuff back up.

04

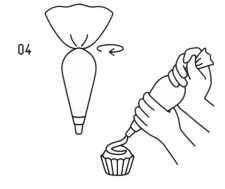

Push all of the buttercream or icing down towards the nozzle, working out any air bubbles, then twist the bag. To pipe, using your dominant hand and keeping an even pressure, squeeze from the top of the bag under the twist. Use your other hand near the nozzle to guide the piping.

PIPING STYLES AND NOZZLES

Children love a cupcake – who doesn't? Here are four of my favourite frosting styles, and the piping nozzles you'll need to create them. Simple and versatile, your cupcakes will not only taste amazing but will look super stylish.

ROUND OPEN SWIRL
Nozzle: 1A

Start at the centre of your cupcake. Apply a little pressure to make a small dollop of buttercream. Do not release the pressure.

Circle the dollop clockwise, working your way around from the centre to the outer edge of the cupcake.

Once the cupcake is covered, without releasing the pressure, make a slightly smaller swirl on top of the first.

Repeat. I like to do three swirls for a nice tall frosting.

DROP STAR
Nozzle: 2D

Start at the outer edge of your cupcake. Pipe a single drop star: apply a little pressure at first, then release the pressure at the end, push in the nozzle and then pull away.

Continue around the edge of the cupcake to make a ring of drop stars.

Make a second ring of drop stars inside the first ring.

Continue until you are at the centre of the cupcake and it is completely covered.

FRENCH TIP SWIRL
Nozzle: 6B

Start at the centre of your cupcake. Apply a little pressure to make a small dollop of buttercream. Do not release the pressure.

Circle the dollop clockwise, working your way around from the centre to the outer edge of the cupcake.

Once the cupcake is covered, without releasing the pressure, make a slightly smaller swirl on top of the first.

Repeat. I like to do three swirls for a nice tall frosting.

ROSETTE
Nozzle: 1M

Start at the centre of your cupcake. Apply a little pressure to make a small dollop of buttercream. Do not release the pressure.

Circle the dollop clockwise, working your way around from the centre to the outer edge of the cupcake.

Keep the pressure throughout the whole swirl, and release at the very end.

2

FROSTINGS AND FILLINGS

There are lots of frostings and fillings out there, and this section includes some of my favourites. You can mix and match them with the cupcake and cake bases in this book to create all sorts of flavour combinations. I love chocolate sponge with a salted caramel buttercream, zesty lemon sponge with a cream cheese frosting, or a simple vanilla sponge with raspberry buttercream. Yum!

Remember that some frostings and fillings are more stable than others. Choccy buttercream, for instance, is better than cream cheese frosting in warmer temperatures. We make masses of frosting every week in the BKD bakery. My son, Cai, is a bit of a buttercream fiend, but any filling you choose will put a delicious finishing touch to your cupcakes and cakes.

FLUFFY BUTTERCREAM

The secret to a lovely fluffy buttercream is patience; mixing on a high speed will incorporate air bubbles and make your buttercream light and fluffy. A simple and delicious topping.

Covers 12–14 cupcakes

INGREDIENTS
200g unsalted butter
450g icing sugar, sifted
2 tbsp milk
flavouring of your choice
food colouring gel
(optional)

TOOLS
- sieve
- electric mixer
- mixing bowl
- spatula
- measuring spoons

Cream together the butter and half the icing sugar for 3–5 minutes until pale and fluffy. Start on a low speed and increase to a medium to high speed.

Add the other half of the icing sugar and mix for a further 2–3 minutes. Start on a low speed and increase to a medium speed.

Scrape down the sides of the bowl with a spatula and add the milk and flavouring. Mix for a final minute at a medium to high speed to ensure the buttercream is well combined. The finished buttercream should be almost white in colour. If you'd like to add colouring, add it at this point.

STORAGE
You can store your buttercream in the fridge for up to one week. Just make sure you let it come to room temperature and give it another mix before using it.

You can also freeze any leftover buttercream for up to three months. Leave overnight in the fridge to thaw, and mix before use.

FLAVOUR OPTIONS
For vanilla buttercream: Add ½–1 tsp vanilla essence.

For raspberry buttercream: Add 3 tbsp seedless raspberry jam.

For lemon buttercream: Add 1 tsp lemon essence or 2 tsp finely grated lemon zest.

For salted caramel buttercream: Add 1½ batches salted caramel sauce (p. 41)

TIP:
To colour your buttercream, add a few drops of food colouring gel until you reach your desired colour.
A cocktail stick can come in handy here, to drop in small amounts.

TIP:
I like to place a clean tea towel over the top of my mixer to prevent clouds of icing sugar covering everything in my kitchen!

CHOCCY BUTTERCREAM

My family loves chocolate. This recipe requires a little extra work but is well worth the effort of adding the melted chocolate. Indulgent, creamy and downright yummy!

Covers 12–14 cupcakes

INGREDIENTS

120g dark chocolate
(70% cocoa solids)
200g unsalted butter
360g icing sugar, sifted
3 tbsp milk

TIP:

Always use dark chocolate. It won't taste bitter in the buttercream, but will give it a nice rich colour and yummy choccy taste.

TOOLS
- sieve
- heatproof bowl
- saucepan
- electric mixer
- mixing bowl
- spatula
- measuring spoons

Set a heatproof bowl over a saucepan of simmering water on a medium heat (bain-marie). Break the chocolate into small pieces and add to the bowl. Stir until the chocolate is completely melted. Set aside to cool a little.

Cream together the butter and half the icing sugar for 3–5 minutes until pale and fluffy. Start on a low speed and increase to a medium to high speed.

Add the other half of the icing sugar and mix for a further 2–3 minutes. Start on a low speed and increase to a medium speed.

Scrape down the sides of the bowl with a spatula and add the milk and cooled melted chocolate. Mix for a final minute at a medium to high speed to ensure the buttercream is well combined and nice and fluffy.

STORAGE

You can store your buttercream in the fridge for up to one week. Just make sure you let it come to room temperature and give it another mix before using it.

You can also freeze any leftover buttercream for up to three months. Leave overnight in the fridge to thaw, and mix before use.

CREAM CHEESE FROSTING

A perfect frosting for those who don't want the sweetness of buttercream. Still creamy but super light. Yum!

Covers 12–14 cupcakes

INGREDIENTS

75g unsalted butter

450g icing sugar, sifted

150g full-fat cream cheese, cold

flavouring of your choice

food colouring gel (optional)

TOOLS	
• electric mixer	• measuring spoons
• mixing bowl	• spatula
• sieve	

Cream together the butter and half the icing sugar for 1–2 minutes until pale and fluffy. Start on a low speed and increase to a medium to high speed.

Add the other half of the icing sugar and a quarter of the cream cheese. Mix for a further 1–2 minutes. Start on a low speed and increase to a medium speed.

Add the rest of the cream cheese, flavouring and colouring gel if you are using it. Mix for a further minute at a medium speed until completely incorporated.

Scrape down the sides of the bowl with a spatula. Mix for a further 2–3 minutes at a medium to high speed until fluffy and almost white in colour (unless you've used food colouring).

TIP:

Make sure you don't overbeat once you add the cream cheese, or your frosting will become runny.

STORAGE

You can store your cream cheese frosting in the fridge for up to one week. Just make sure you let it come to room temperature and give it another mix before using it.

You can also freeze any leftover cream cheese frosting for up to three months. Leave overnight in the fridge to thaw, and mix before use.

TIP:

I prefer to use zest. As it's finely grated, the kids won't spot it!

FLAVOUR OPTIONS

For vanilla cream cheese frosting: Add ½–1 tsp vanilla essence.

For chocolate cream cheese frosting: Add 45g cocoa powder.

For chocolate orange cream cheese frosting: Add 45g cocoa powder and 1 tsp orange essence or 2 tsp finely grated orange zest.

For lemon cream cheese frosting: Add 1 tsp lemon essence or 2 tsp finely grated lemon zest.

ROYAL ICING

Use this to pipe messages, draw patterns on cookies, stick cakes to cake boards, and to hold your gingerbread houses together.

Makes approximately 300g

INGREDIENTS

white of 1 medium
    free-range egg
2 tsp lemon juice
250g icing sugar, sifted
food colouring gel
    (optional)

TOOLS

- sieve
- measuring spoons
- electric mixer
- mixing bowl
- spatula

Mix the egg white, lemon juice and icing sugar together for about 1–2 minutes on a low speed.

Scrape down the sides of the bowl with a spatula. Add the food colouring gel if you are using it, and give it a final mix for 30 seconds to ensure the icing is well combined. Add a little extra lemon juice if you find your icing is too stiff.

STORAGE

You can store your royal icing in the fridge for up to two days in an airtight container. Placing cling film on the surface of the royal icing prevents it from forming a skin.

TIP:

You can buy royal icing powder from supermarkets if you prefer. You just add water.

CHOCOLATE GANACHE

This is great as a filling or drizzled over your cupcakes. For a vibrant twist, use white chocolate tinted with food colouring gels inside your cupcakes or drizzled over the top of a cake, à la Katherine Sabbath.

Fills 12–14 cupcakes

INGREDIENTS

100ml double cream

200g dark chocolate (70% cocoa solids), milk chocolate or white chocolate

food colouring gel (optional – use with white chocolate)

TIP:

If you want coloured chocolate, use white chocolate and add a few drops of food colouring gel at a time until you reach your desired colour. Mix in when the chocolate is hot and runny. Add a little vegetable shortening if it's too thick.

TOOLS
- measuring jug
- heatproof bowl
- saucepan
- spatula

Set a heatproof bowl over a saucepan of simmering water on a medium heat (bain-marie). Add the cream and stir with a spatula until it is hot.

Break the chocolate into small pieces and add to the cream. Stir until the chocolate is completely melted.

Remove from the hob and stir in the food colouring gel if you are using it. Allow to cool for about 10 minutes before filling your cupcakes.

STORAGE

Chocolate ganache can be stored in the fridge for up to two weeks in an airtight container. Placing cling film on the surface of the ganache prevents it from forming a skin.

SALTED CARAMEL SAUCE

A super-simple and yummy way to pimp up your cupcakes! Use it to fill or drizzle over your cupcakes, or add to your frosting. I could eat this stuff by the barrel-load!

Fills 12–24 cupcakes

INGREDIENTS
125ml double cream
½ tsp vanilla essence
3 tbsp water
120g caster sugar
½ tsp of flaked sea salt

TIP:

If you find you have a few lumps, reheat the sauce on a very low heat.

TOOLS
- measuring jug
- measuring spoons
- saucepan
- spatula

Measure the double cream in a jug and add the vanilla essence. Stir and set aside.

Pour the water and caster sugar into a saucepan and stir with a spatula.

Put on a medium to high heat for 6–10 minutes. Do not stir, but you can swirl the pan to make sure all the sugar melts. The sugar will start to dissolve, bubble and turn a deep amber colour. Remove from the hob.

Gradually add the double cream, stirring continuously with a spatula.

Add the flaked sea salt, crushing it in with your fingers. Stir well. Allow to cool for 10–15 minutes before filling your cupcakes. You can also add this to my buttercream recipe (p. 32) or use as a drizzle on top of your cakes.

STORAGE

I normally make big batches of this yummy stuff. It can be stored in the fridge for up to two weeks in an airtight container. Reheat to get a runnier texture if using after refrigerating.

3

CUPCAKES

I used to hang out with my nan, Nanny Fowler, most weekends growing up, and we loved baking, knitting and rummaging around a car boot sale. Pretty teacups and saucers were my favourite thing to collect. These days, I love nothing better than having a nice cuppa, in a proper teacup, with a delicious zesty lemon cupcake.

Children can't resist cupcakes, and they're always a big hit with our BKD mini bakers. In this section I've picked out some of my favourite cupcake and cake-pop creations, including my signature rainbow unicorn cupcake, which was originally inspired by my stepdaughter Elsie's love of unicorns, and some irresistibly cute and super-spooky treats too.

VANILLA CUPCAKES

Light and fluffy cupcakes, the perfect base to many of my creations.

Makes 12 large cupcakes

INGREDIENTS

200g unsalted butter

200g caster sugar

2 tsp vanilla essence

4 medium free-range eggs, lightly beaten

200g self-raising flour, sifted

TIP:

I like to use a tablespoon to scoop up my batter, and a teaspoon to push it into the cupcake cases.

TIP:

Always use eggs at room temperature to prevent your mixture curdling.

TOOLS

- 12-hole muffin tin
- cupcake cases
- sieve
- measuring spoons
- electric mixer
- mixing bowl
- spatula
- wire rack

PREPARE

Preheat the oven to 180°C/350°F/gas 4. Line the muffin tin with cupcake cases.

MIX

Cream the butter, sugar and vanilla essence together for about 5 minutes until pale and fluffy. Start on a low speed and gradually increase.

Add the eggs to the butter and sugar mixture little by little, to avoid curdling. Add a little flour if you notice the mixture splitting. Mix on a low speed now, and for the remainder of the mixing.

Mix in the rest of the flour.

Scrape down the sides of the bowl with a spatula and give the batter a final mix.

BAKE

Fill the cupcake cases two-thirds full and bake for 16–18 minutes or until golden brown. To check your cupcakes are well baked, insert a cake tester or cocktail stick – it should come out clean. They should also feel springy to the touch. Leave to cool a little, then transfer to a wire rack.

STORAGE

These are best eaten on the day they're baked, but can be stored in an airtight container for up to three days once cool.

FLAVOUR OPTIONS

For lemon cupcakes: Substitute vanilla essence with 2 tsp lemon essence or 5 tsp finely grated lemon zest.

CHOCCY CUPCAKES

Super-chocolatey cupcakes are perfect paired with my yummy salted caramel buttercream. One for the chocolate fiends!

Makes 12 large cupcakes

INGREDIENTS

200g unsalted butter

200g caster sugar

4 medium free-range eggs, lightly beaten

150g self-raising flour, sifted

70g cocoa powder, sifted

TOOLS

- 12-hole muffin tin
- cupcake cases
- sieve
- electric mixer
- mixing bowl
- measuring spoons
- spatula
- wire rack

PREPARE

Preheat the oven to 180°C/350°F/gas 4. Line a muffin tin with cupcake cases.

MIX

Cream the butter and sugar together for about 5 minutes until pale and fluffy. Start on a low speed and gradually increase.

Add the eggs to the butter and sugar mixture little by little, to avoid curdling. Add a little flour if you notice the mixture splitting. Mix on a low speed now, and for the remainder of the mixing.

Mix in the rest of the flour and all the cocoa powder.

Scrape down the sides of the bowl with a spatula and give the batter a final mix.

BAKE

Fill the cupcake cases two-thirds full and bake for 16–18 minutes. They should feel springy to the touch when cooked. Leave to cool a little, then transfer to a wire rack.

STORAGE

These are best eaten on the day they're baked, but can be stored in an airtight container for up to three days once cool.

FLAVOUR OPTIONS

For chocolate orange cupcakes: Add 2 tsp orange essence or 5 tsp finely grated orange zest. I also like to add small chunks of orange-flavoured chocolate – yum!

RAINBOW UNICORN CUPCAKES

This magical cupcake creature is a mini-baker favourite. It was originally inspired by Elsie's love of unicorns and is an equal hit with girls and boys. The perfect addition to any rainbow-themed party.

Makes 12 large cupcakes

FOR THE CUPCAKE BASES

1 batch vanilla or lemon cupcakes (p. 45) in silver cupcake cases

FOR THE BUTTERCREAM FROSTING

1 batch buttercream (p. 32) or cream cheese frosting (p. 35)

food colouring gels in rainbow colours

TO DECORATE

icing sugar or cornflour, for rolling out

140g white sugarpaste

6 large white marshmallows

black edible ink pen or black food colouring gel

edible candy eyes

edible glitter (optional)

TOOLS

- non-stick mat
- silicone rolling pin
- petal cookie cutter
- blunt knife
- plastic piping bag
- scissors
- piping nozzle (2D star tip)
- paintbrush size 6, for rainbow food colouring
- measuring cup
- paintbrush size 00 or black edible ink pen, for nostrils

I would suggest starting with the sugarcraft work for the unicorns before baking the cupcakes or making the frosting. This will allow some time for hardening. If you can leave overnight, even better!

SUGARCRAFT

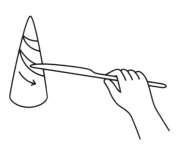

01 Dust the non-stick mat with a little icing sugar or cornflour. Using the silicone rolling pin, roll out the white sugarpaste to approximately 4mm in thickness. Cut 24 petal shapes for the unicorns' ears. Pinch the wider ends together.

02 Use the remaining white sugarpaste to make 12 unicorn horns. Roll a small piece of white sugarpaste in the palms of your hands to make cone shapes. Make them around 4–4.5cm long and ensure the bases are wide enough for them to stand up on the non-stick mat. Repeat the process 12 times.

Take the blunt side of a knife and gently press it around the horns from tip to bottom to make a spiral indent.

Leave the sugarpaste shapes to dry and harden.

MAKE THE CUPCAKES

Prepare and bake the vanilla or lemon cupcakes.

MAKE THE RAINBOW FROSTING

01   Make a batch of your chosen frosting. Prepare your piping bag with a 2D star tip nozzle.

02   Line up the food gels in rainbow order: ROYGBIV. Dip the paintbrush into the red pot first, then paint a line down the inside of the piping bag from top to bottom. Paint twice, along the same line. Do the same for each of the other colours, leaving a gap of about 2cm between each one, around the whole of the piping bag.

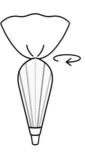

TIP:

Don't worry if you accidentally get a little food colouring on the wrong part of the piping bag. It won't show when you pipe the cupcakes.

03   Once you have finished painting the piping bag, fill it with the frosting. Using a measuring cup, scoop up the frosting and drop it into the bag. Shake the bag, holding the top with two hands so as not to disturb the food colouring too much. Keep adding the frosting and shaking until your bag is full.

04   Gently press the bag to ensure no air is trapped and that the frosting is right at the bottom. Twist the top of the bag and pipe the frosting through the nozzle until you start to see the rainbow effect. Set your piping bag aside.

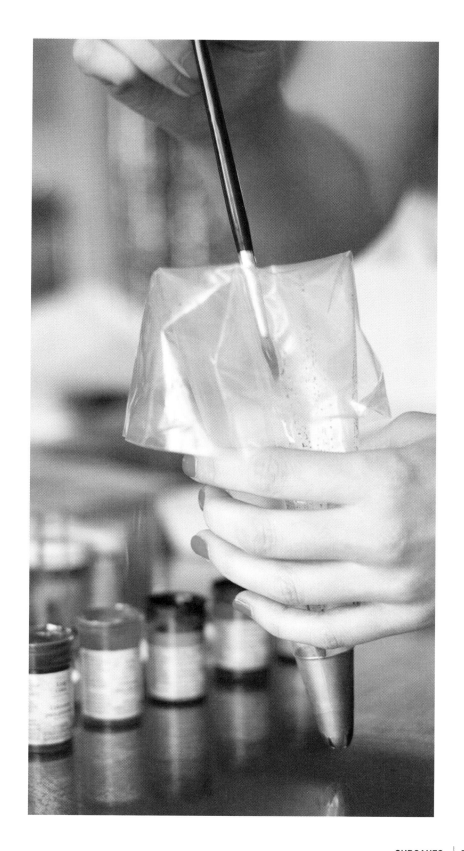

CREATE THE UNICORN CUPCAKES

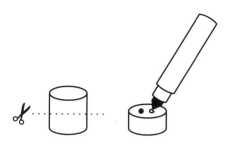

01 If necessary, slice off the top of the cupcakes so they are nice and flat.

02 Cut the large marshmallows in half and draw on two nostrils with a black edible ink pen, or use a thin paintbrush and black food colouring gel.

03 Take the rainbow frosting. Decorate each cupcake using the rosette technique (p. 29). I like to use this style as it gives a flatter finish.

04 Add the marshmallow noses at the bottom centre of each cupcake.

05 Next, place two edible candy eyes just above each nose. Remember to leave enough room for the unicorn's ears.

06 Add the ears, ensuring you stick them firmly into the frosting. Position them so they are slightly upright – they stay in place better that way.

07 Finally, add the unicorns' horns. Again, push these in really firmly so they don't topple over. If you wish, you can also sprinkle your unicorns with edible glitter for that extra little magical sparkle!

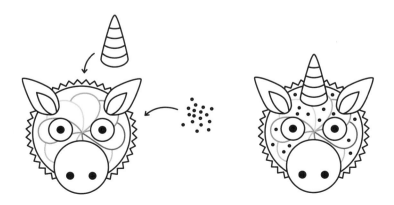

HAPPY BURGER CUPCAKES

The cutest burger you'll ever eat and always a big hit with kids! They are perfect for any American diner-style party.

Makes 12 cupcakes

FOR THE CUPCAKE BURGERS

1½ batches choccy cupcake mix (p. 47)

FOR THE CUPCAKE BUNS

2 batches vanilla cupcake mix (p. 45)

FOR THE BUTTERCREAM TOMATO SAUCE

½ batch buttercream (p. 32)

red food colouring gel

TO DECORATE

85g yellow sugarpaste

15g orange sugarpaste

icing sugar or cornflour, for dusting

170g green sugarpaste

apricot jam

popping candy

black icing writer or ½ batch royal icing (p.38) coloured with black food colouring gel

24 edible candy eyes

TOOLS

- 23cm x 32cm (9in x 13in) rectangular cake tin
- baking parchment
- 5cm circular cutter
- 12-hole muffin tin
- non-stick cooking spray
- measuring spoons
- plastic piping bag or squeezy tomato sauce bottle
- scissors
- non-stick mat
- silicone rolling pin
- 5cm square cookie cutter (optional)
- sugarcraft knife
- template (p. 150)
- cupcake corer or apple corer (optional)
- paintbrush
- 12 mini skewers
- mini burger boxes (optional)

MAKE THE BURGERS

Preheat the oven to 150°C/300°F/gas 2. Line the cake tin. Prepare the choccy cupcake mix, then pour into the lined tin and bake for 23–25 minutes. Allow to cool for about 10 minutes and then cut out 12 cakes using the 5cm circular cutter. Use your hands to crumble the edges a little so they look more like burgers.

MAKE THE BUNS

Increase the oven heat to 160°C/325°F/gas 3. Prepare the vanilla cupcake mix. Spray the muffin tin with non-stick cooking spray and fill with half the cupcake mix. I find one slightly heaped tablespoon of mix in each hole works best. Bake for 15–17 minutes or until golden brown. Repeat with the remaining cupcake mix to make a second batch of vanilla cupcakes, so you have 24 buns.

MAKE THE TOMATO SAUCE

Make the buttercream and colour with red food colouring gel. Snip a small hole at the end of the piping bag using scissors and fill the bag with the buttercream – you don't need a nozzle. You can also use a squeezy tomato sauce bottle for this. Kids will love to do the squeezing!

SUGARCRAFT

Unlike some of the other projects in this book, you don't need to make the sugarcraft elements ahead of time for drying. I like my lettuce and cheese to have a bit of flop!

TIP:

Remember to push the cookie cutter firmly into the mat and give it a little wiggle to ensure you get nice clean lines on your sugarpaste.

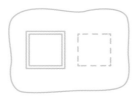

01 Mix a small amount of orange sugarpaste with the yellow sugarpaste to get your desired cheese colour. I like a slight orange tint.

Dust the non-stick mat with a little icing sugar or cornflour. Using the silicone rolling pin, roll out some of the sugarpaste to about 3–4mm in thickness.

Cut 12 sugarpaste cheese squares using a 5cm square cookie cutter or a sugarcraft knife. Set aside.

TIP:

For a quicker option, you can make a yellow buttercream for mustard and skip the cheese and lettuce sugarcraft.

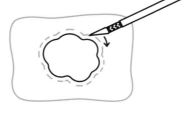

02 Dust the non-stick mat with a little icing sugar or cornflour. Using the silicone rolling pin, roll out some of the green sugarpaste to about 3–4mm in thickness.

Using a sugarcraft knife and the lettuce template, cut 12 pieces of lettuce. Feel free to make them all slightly different – the template is just a guide.

Run the pad of your index finger around the lettuce pieces to thin the edges. Set aside for about 5 minutes to let them firm up a little.

CREATE THE BURGER CUPCAKES

TIP:

I use a cupcake corer or apple corer to remove part of the inside of the bottom cupcake and fill it with a little extra buttercream.

01 Take 12 vanilla cupcakes. Squeeze a small amount of red buttercream on the top centre of each one. Take care not to go too close to the sides.

02 Place the choccy burgers on top. The buttercream will help them stick.

03 Place a sugarpaste lettuce leaf on top of each burger. Then place a sugarpaste cheese square on top of the lettuce.

04 Squeeze a zigzag of red buttercream across the top of the cheese to look like tomato sauce.

05 Take the 12 remaining vanilla cupcakes and turn them upside down. Using a paintbrush, brush the top of each one with a little apricot jam. Then sprinkle with popping candy. Place the vanilla cupcakes on top of the buttercream tomato sauce.

06 Stick a mini skewer through the middle to hold everything firmly together.

FINISH

01 Using a black icing writer or black royal icing, attach two eyes to each cupcake burger.

02 Now draw a smiley mouth.

Place in a mini burger box and enjoy!

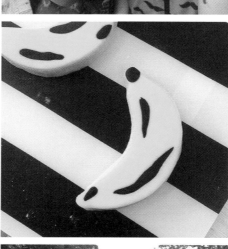

SPOOKY CUPCAKES

No trick, all treat spooky cupcakes! We love Halloween in our house. These yummy chocolate and salted caramel cupcakes go down a storm. BOO!

Makes 12 large cupcakes

FOR THE CUPCAKE BASES

1 batch choccy cupcakes
   (p. 47) in black and
   purple foil cupcake cases

FOR THE BUTTERCREAM FROSTING

1½ batches buttercream
   (p. 32)
icing whitener (optional)
purple food colouring gel

FOR THE FILLING

1 batch salted caramel
   sauce (p. 41)

TO DECORATE

icing sugar or cornflour,
   for dusting
85g black sugarpaste
10g red sugarpaste
6 white mini
   marshmallows
edible glue or
   white icing writer
edible candy eyes
edible glitter (optional)

TOOLS

- non-stick mat
- silicone rolling pin
- 7cm circular cookie cutter
- sugarcraft knife
- 4cm circular fondant cutter
- 1cm circular fondant cutter (optional)
- scissors
- paintbrush
- two piping bags
- piping nozzles (bat – 2D star tip / ghost – 1A round flat)
- cupcake corer or apple corer
- teaspoon

I would suggest starting with the sugarcraft work for the bats before baking the cupcakes or making the buttercream and filling. If possible, make the bat wings and mouths the day before to allow them maximum time for drying. Otherwise you may get floppy wings!

MAKE THE CUPCAKES

Prepare and bake the choccy cupcakes.

MAKE THE FROSTING

Make the buttercream and split it into two piping bags. Take two-thirds for the ghosts – I like to add a whitener for a brighter white buttercream – and fit a 1A round flat nozzle. For the bats, colour the remaining third purple with the food colouring gel and fit a 2D star tip nozzle.

MAKE THE FILLING

Make the salted caramel sauce.

FILL THE CUPCAKES

Use a cupcake corer or apple corer to remove the centres of the cupcakes. Fill each one with salted caramel sauce. I like to use a piping bag to do this, but you can also use a teaspoon. Fill to just over halfway. Avoid over-filling or the salted caramel will mix with the buttercream. You can also top with a little leftover cupcake to keep the two separate.

CREATE THE BAT CUPCAKES

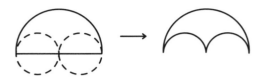

SUGARCRAFT

01   Dust the non-stick mat with a little icing sugar or cornflour. Using the silicone rolling pin, roll out some of the black fondant to about 3–4mm in thickness. Take a 7cm circular cookie cutter and cut six circles. Then use the sugarcraft knife to cut them all in half to make 12 wings.

02   Next take a 4cm circular sugarpaste cutter and cut two semicircles along the straight edge of each wing. Ensure that each curve lines up to make a point. Repeat for all the wings.

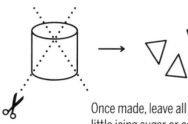

03   Dust the non-stick mat with a little more icing sugar or cornflour. Using the silicone rolling pin, roll out the red fondant to about 3–4mm in thickness. Use a 1cm circular cookie cutter and cut six circles. Take the sugarcraft knife and cut a straight edge a quarter of the way down. Discard the small piece, then stretch the fondant slightly lengthways to make a mouth shape. You can also cut this by hand if you don't have a cutter small enough.

04   Use a pair of scissors to cut the mini marshmallows into tiny triangles. You'll need two per mouth. Attach with a little edible glue on a paintbrush, or a white icing writer.

Once made, leave all your sugarpaste parts to dry on a non-stick mat dusted with a little icing sugar or cornflour.

PIPING

Decorate each cupcake with purple buttercream, using the drop star technique (p. 28). I like to use this style to get a furry effect.

FINISH

01   Place the red fanged mouth at the very bottom of the cupcake, in the centre.

TIP:

If leaving overnight, leave exposed to the air on a non-stick mat or baking parchment. Sprinkle it with icing sugar or cornflour first so they don't stick.

TIP:

I like to add a sprinkle of edible glitter over the top of the bats or on their wings using edible glue or a little water to make the sugarpaste sticky.

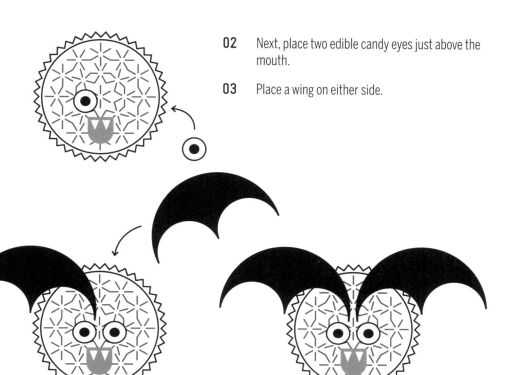

02   Next, place two edible candy eyes just above the mouth.

03   Place a wing on either side.

TIP:

These super-simple ghost cupcakes are great to make with younger children.

CREATE THE GHOST CUPCAKES

SUGARCRAFT

01   Take a small amount of black fondant. Roll 12 small balls for the eyes.

02   Next, roll six slightly larger balls for the mouths. Then flatten them between your thumb and index finger.

PIPING

Decorate each cupcake with white buttercream, using the round open swirl technique (p. 28).

FINISH

Place the eyes and mouth as shown in the illustration. Gently press them on – the buttercream will act as glue.

You're done – mwa, ha, ha, ha!

ICE CREAM SUNDAE CAKE POPS

A perfect summer party treat and no worrying about them melting! I love filling the cones with treats too, for an extra little sunny surprise.

Makes 10

FOR THE CAKE POPS

½ batch choccy cupcakes (p. 47) or make a whole batch and have some leftovers for the kids to nibble on

2 batches chocolate ganache (p. 39)

TO DECORATE

10 ice cream cones

chocolate beans (optional)

mini marshmallows (optional)

1 bag white candy melts

electric pink food colouring gel

vegetable shortening (optional)

sprinkles

FOR OPTIONAL GLITTERED CHERRIES

fresh cherries

edible glitter

edible glue

paintbrush

TOOLS

- baking sheet
- baking parchment or non-stick mat
- mixing bowl
- spatula
- tablespoon
- short glass tumblers
- heatproof bowl
- saucepan

MAKE THE CUPCAKES

Prepare and bake the choccy cupcakes. I like to make them the day before so they're not so soft.

MAKE THE CHOCOLATE GANACHE

Make the chocolate ganache and allow to cool for 5–10 minutes. Keep the bain-marie to one side as you may need it to reheat the ganache later.

CREATE THE CAKE POPS

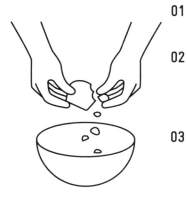

01   Line a baking sheet with baking parchment or a non-stick mat.

02   Remove six cupcakes from their cupcake cases and crumble into a mixing bowl. Add half the chocolate ganache and mix with a spatula until well combined.

03   Take a heaped tablespoon of cake-pop mix and roll into a ball in the palms of your hands. Repeat this until you have ten balls and have used all of the mix. Place the cake-pop balls on the lined baking sheet. Chill in the fridge for about 30 minutes, or for 15 minutes in the freezer.

04   Reheat the ganache if it's thickening, and pour a little around the inside of each cone. Place the cones in short glass tumblers to hold them upright.

05 Half fill the cones with chocolate beans and marshmallows if you're using them.

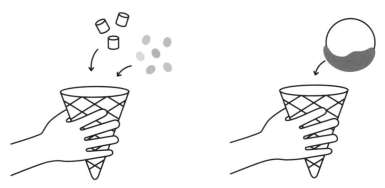

06 Take the cake-pop balls out of the fridge. Dip the end of each ball into the chocolate ganache. Push the balls on top of the cones firmly, chocolate-side down. Put back into the fridge for another hour, until really firm.

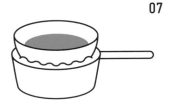

07 Set a heatproof bowl over a saucepan of simmering water on a medium heat (bain-marie). Add the candy melts to the bowl and stir for 2–3 minutes until melted.

Add your choice of food colouring gel a drop at a time, until you have your desired colour. I use electric pink.

TiP:

You can also heat the candy melts in a microwave, stirring every 20 seconds until completely melted. If the candy melts feel too thick, add a little vegetable shortening.

08 Remove the cake pops from the fridge – they should feel firm. Take each one and dip it in the candy melts to coat the top. Feel free to add some sprinkles at this point too.

09 Allow the candy melt coating to set. It will set a lot quicker than the ganache did, in around 2–5 minutes. If you plan to add a glittered cherry, prepare these now. Once the candy melt coating has set, rewarm any chocolate ganache you have left and spoon a little over the top.

Add sprinkles whilst the chocolate ganache is still wet. You'll need the chocolate ganache to still be wet when you add the cherry on top.

OPTIONAL

An ice cream sundae isn't complete without a cherry on top! For a quick option, add a red chocolate bean on top. For a more glitzy version, take fresh cherries and paint them with edible glue. Allow to dry for about 1 minute and then shake edible glitter all over. Pop one on top of each of your ice cream sundae cake pops. Yay!

CAKES

My love of baking started with cakes. I remember the first ever celebration cake I made – a fruitcake, covered in buttercream and sweets. I was so proud! Birthdays are always an excuse for me to get my apron on. I've made cakes for our children and for siblings, cousins, partners, friends and work colleagues over the years.

This section will help you create something with real wow factor for the people you love – stunning cakes for every occasion. I first made the dino cake for my dino-loving boy's third birthday party, and children always go mad for the hidden sweetie surprise in the rainbow funfetti piñata cake.

VANILLA SPONGE CAKE

For a classic vanilla sponge cake, fill with vanilla buttercream and raspberry jam. Swap the vanilla flavouring and you have lots of other flavour options too. I like making my cakes tall, and this three-layer cake is the perfect party size.

Makes a three-layer 20cm (8in) cake

INGREDIENTS

900g unsalted butter

900g caster sugar

3 tbsp vanilla essence

18 medium free-range eggs, lightly beaten

900g self-raising flour, sifted

filling of your choice

TOOLS

- 3 x 20cm (8in) cake tins
- baking parchment
- pencil
- scissors
- sieve
- electric mixer
- mixing bowl
- measuring spoons
- spatula
- cup scoop
- wire rack
- cake-cutting wire

TIP:

If you choose to use one cake tin, make the mix three times: leaving the cake batter in the bowl for too long will affect the end result.

TIP:

Always use eggs at room temperature to prevent your mixture curdling.

PREPARE

Preheat the oven to 160°C/325°F/gas 3. Line the cake tins.

If you have a standard-size oven you can bake two layers in two cake tins first and then follow with the third layer in a third tin. Make the mix for the third layer whilst the others are baking.

If you only have one cake tin, you can divide the recipe by three and bake three cakes, one after the other. Allow enough time, as obviously this will take longer.

MIX

Cream the butter, caster sugar and vanilla essence together for about 5 minutes until pale and fluffy. Start on a low speed and gradually increase.

Add the eggs little by little, to avoid curdling. Add a little flour if you notice the mixture splitting. Mix on a low speed now, and for the remainder of the mixing.

Mix in the rest of the flour.

Scrape down the sides of the bowl with a spatula and give the batter a final mix.

Fill the cake tins.

BAKE

Bake for about 35–45 minutes if baking one layer or 45–55 minutes for two, or until golden brown. The cakes should be coming away from the sides of the tins and feel springy to the touch. To check the cakes are well baked, insert a cake tester or cocktail stick. It should come out clean.

Leave the cakes to cool in their tins for about 10 minutes. Then carefully turn them out, remove the baking parchment and leave them to cool fully on a wire rack.

When cooled, take a knife or cake-cutting wire and level the top of each tier. Then sandwich them together with a filling of your choice.

STORAGE

Cakes can be stored in an airtight container for up to three days once cool.

FLAVOUR OPTIONS

For lemon cakes: Substitute vanilla essence with 3 tbsp lemon essence or the finely grated zest of 13 lemons and the juice of five lemons (about 5 tbsp). Increase the baking time by 5–10 minutes – or as long as it takes for the cakes to turn a lovely golden brown.

TIP:

I like to bake cakes the day before decorating them. Once they are cool, I wrap the cakes in cling film to allow them to firm, and then level and sandwich them together the next day, when they're less crumbly. This also helps when you're busy with the kids and doing a million and one things!

**Makes a two-layer
25cm (10in) cake**

INGREDIENTS

260g dark chocolate
(70% cocoa solids)

800g unsalted butter

800g caster sugar

16 medium free-range eggs,
lightly beaten

600g self-raising flour,
sifted

300g cocoa powder, sifted

TIP:

**Bang the cake tin lightly
on the work surface before
putting the cake into the
oven. This prevents any
large air holes forming in
the sponge.**

CHOCCY BROWNIE CAKE

This cake is chocolate heaven and a recipe I often use in the bakery. It's best
slightly underbaked for that fudgy, melt-in-your-mouth texture.

TOOLS		
• 2 x 25cm (10in) cake tins	• heatproof bowl	• spatula
• baking parchment	• saucepan	• cup scoop
• pencil	• electric mixer	• wire rack
• scissors	• mixing bowl	• cake-cutting wire
	• sieve	

PREPARE

Preheat the oven to 160°C/325°F/gas 3. Line the cake tins.

Divide the recipe by two and bake two cakes, one after the other. Make the mix twice,
as leaving the cake batter in the bowl for too long will affect the end result.

MIX

Set a heatproof bowl over a saucepan of simmering water on a medium heat (bain-
marie). Break the chocolate into small pieces and place in the bowl. Stir until the
chocolate is completely melted. Set aside.

Cream the butter and caster sugar together for about 5 minutes until pale and fluffy.
Start on a low speed and gradually increase.

Add the eggs little by little, to avoid curdling. Add a little flour if you notice the mixture
splitting. Mix on a low speed now, and for the remainder of the mixing.

Mix in the rest of the flour and all the cocoa powder.

Scrape down the sides of the bowl with a spatula, pour in the melted chocolate
and give the batter a final mix.

Fill the cake tins.

BAKE

Bake each cake for about 55–60 minutes. The cakes should be coming away from
the sides of the tins and feel springy to the touch. To check the cakes are ready,
insert a cake tester or cocktail stick. It should come out slightly wet. For a fudgy
brownie texture, this cake is best slightly underbaked.

Leave the cakes to cool in their tins for about 10 minutes. Then carefully turn them out, remove the baking parchment and leave them to cool fully on a wire rack.

When cooled, take a knife or cake-cutting wire and level the top of each tier. Then sandwich them together with a filling of your choice. I love using a salted caramel buttercream filling (p. 32). Or how about chocolate orange cream cheese frosting (p. 35)?

STORAGE

Cakes can be stored in an airtight container for up to three days once cool.

GIANT MONSTER CUPCAKE CAKE

What could be better than a giant cupcake? Your little monsters will love this 'scary' hairy 3-D monster creation.

Makes one giant cupcake cake

FOR THE CAKE

⅓ batch vanilla sponge cake mix (p. 78)

FOR THE BUTTERCREAM FROSTING

1 batch buttercream (p. 32) for the bottom section of the cake and 1½ for the top

royal blue food colouring gel

lemon yellow food colouring gel

TO DECORATE

icing sugar or cornflour, for dusting

450g white sugarpaste

12g turquoise-blue sugarpaste

12g green sugarpaste

60g black sugarpaste

large white marshmallows

TOOLS

- non-stick mat
- silicone rolling pin
- 4cm circular sugarpaste cutter
- 2cm circular sugarpaste cutter
- paintbrush
- two cake-pop sticks

- sugarcraft knife
- template (p. 150)
- scissors
- non-stick giant cupcake tin
- non-stick cooking spray
- wire rack

- piping bag with a large 235 nozzle
- baking parchment
- turntable
- palette knife
- offset spatula
- 20cm (8in) black circular cake board

Start with the sugarcraft work before baking the cakes or making the buttercream. If possible, make the sugarcraft elements 24 hours before you need them, to allow enough time for drying.

SUGARCRAFT

EYES

01 Take half the white sugarpaste and roll it into two balls of about 6.5cm in diameter. Try to get the finish as smooth as you can. These will be the monster's eyeballs.

02 Dust the non-stick mat with a little icing sugar or cornflour. Using the silicone rolling pin, roll out the turquoise-blue sugarpaste to about 3–4mm in thickness. Cut one sugarpaste circle using the 4cm circular sugarpaste cutter. Repeat the process with the green sugarpaste to cut a second circle. These will be the irises.

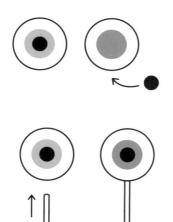

03 Dust the non-stick mat with a little more icing sugar or cornflour and roll out some of the black sugarpaste to about 3–4mm in thickness. Cut two black pupils for the eyes using a 2cm circular sugarpaste cutter.

04 Brush the underside of the green and blue sugarpaste circles with a little water on a paintbrush. Stick one circle in the centre of each eyeball. In the same way, stick one black sugarpaste circle in the centre of each of the coloured circles.

05 Push the cake-pop sticks into the bottom of each eyeball, in the middle. Take care not to push too hard or they will poke through the other side. Set aside to dry.

MOUTH

01 Dust the non-stick mat with a little icing sugar or cornflour. Using the silicone rolling pin, roll out the remaining black sugarpaste to about 4–5mm in thickness. Using the oval mouth template as a guide – although you can cut any shape mouth you like! – cut the sugarpaste using a sugarcraft knife.

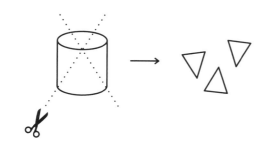

02 Once the mouth has firmed up a little, you can add the marshmallow teeth – as many as you like! Use a pair of scissors to cut triangles from a couple of large marshmallows. Attach the teeth to the mouth using the sticky side of the marshmallow.

Once made, leave all the sugarpaste parts to dry on a non-stick mat dusted with a little icing sugar or cornflour. Do not cover, as they need exposure to the air to harden.

MAKE THE CAKE

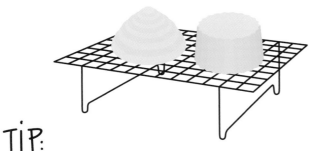

Preheat the oven to 140°C/275°F/gas 1. Make the vanilla sponge cake mix.

Spray non-stick spray all over the insides of the two sections of the giant cupcake tin. Fill the base section of the cake tin first, leaving a gap of approximately 2.5cm at the top. Bake for 15 minutes. Add the rest of the mix to the top cupcake section – there should be a gap of about 2cm at the top. Bake with the base section for a further 40–50 minutes.

Allow the cakes to cool for about 25 minutes in the tins. Place the wire rack on top of each tin and flip them over, then give them a hard tap on the work surface to help release the cakes.

TIP:

Do not leave the cakes in the tin for any longer than 25 minutes or they may start to sweat and stick to the tin.

MAKE THE FROSTING

Make the buttercream. Colour one batch with royal blue food colouring gel and put aside. Colour one and a half batches with lemon yellow food colouring gel and place this in a piping bag fitted with a large 235 nozzle.

TIP:

A 235 nozzle is perfect for creating hair or grass. Have fun experimenting with different nozzles for different effects!

COVER THE CAKE WITH BUTTERCREAM

01   Take the cake base and turn it upside down on top of a piece of baking parchment on the turntable. You won't need to do a crumb coating on this cake. Cover the sides of the cake base in a generous coating of the blue buttercream using a palette knife or offset spatula. Set a small amount aside for step **05**. Take care not to press too hard or spread too thinly, or crumbs will show in the buttercream. Create a smooth layer all the way around.

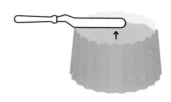

02 To create the crease marks of a cupcake case, take the offset spatula and very gently brush the sides of the cake base from bottom to top to make small grooves in the buttercream. Rotate the turntable and work your way around the whole base.

03 You'll be left with excess buttercream at the top rim of the cake base. Use the offset spatula to draw the edges into the top centre of the cake. Remove the excess on the top of the cake.

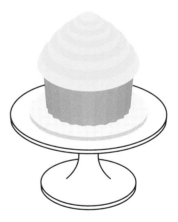

04 Place the cake board on top of the cupcake base. The bottom of the cake board should be facing upwards. Then place one hand on top of the cake board with your fingers spread, and your other hand under the turntable. Tip the cake over so the wider part is at the top.

05 Place the cake, now on its cake board, back on the turntable. Cover the top of the cupcake base with blue buttercream using the offset spatula or palette knife. Take the cupcake top and place it on the base.

06 Cover the cupcake top in plenty of yellow buttercream – it will look like a wobbly haystack. Next, pipe short strands of yellow buttercream to make the monster's fur. Starting at the bottom of the cupcake top, where it meets the blue base, work all the way around the outside. Once that circle is complete, move further up the cupcake top and create another circle of buttercream strands, slightly overlapping the previous one.

Keep working your way up until you are at the top and the whole cupcake top is covered in yellow buttercream fur.

FINISH

Place the mouth on first. To position the eyes, push the cake-pop sticks into the cupcake top, which will support and hold them in place.

Now . . . run for your life!

RAINBOW FUNFETTI PIÑATA CAKE

This celebration cake has it all going on. On the outside it's a colourful burst of rainbow sprinkle fun. Cut into the cake to reveal a sweet surprise and pretty funfetti sponge layers. Rainbow-licious!

Makes a 20cm (8in) cake

FOR THE CAKE

1 batch vanilla sponge cake mix (p. 78)

FOR THE BUTTERCREAM FROSTING

2 batches buttercream (p. 32)

TO FILL AND DECORATE

approx 500g rainbow sprinkles

approx 200g dolly mixture

15g jelly beans

10–15g mini marshmallows

5–10g silver star sprinkles

Any other sweets you may want to use

TOOLS

- 3 x 20cm (8in) non-stick cake tins
- baking parchment
- pencil
- scissors
- 8cm circular cutter
- 20cm (8in) silver circular cake board
- turntable
- palette knife
- offset spatula
- side scraper

MAKE THE CAKE

Prepare the vanilla sponge cake, lightly mixing 9 tbsp rainbow sprinkles into the batter before baking.

MAKE THE FROSTING

Make the buttercream.

CREATE THE PIÑATA CAKE

01

Use the 8cm circular cutter to cut a circle out of the middle of two cake layers. Stick the first layer to the centre of the cake board and sandwich the second on top with buttercream.

02 Mix and add a variety of small sweets to the hole in the cake. I use dolly mixture, jelly beans, mini marshmallows and star sprinkles. Put plenty into the hole, filling it until the sweets are 5–8mm from the top.

03 Evenly spread the second cake layer with buttercream. Take care not to put buttercream over the sweets.

TIP:

You can gently shape the top edges of the cake with the tips of your fingers to give a nice sharp finish after you've added the sprinkles.

04 Sandwich the final cake layer on top.

05 Place the cake on a turntable. Crumb coat the cake (p. 24).

06 Cover the cake in buttercream, using a palette knife, then a side scraper to give a smooth finish. It doesn't need to be completely perfect as it will be coated with sprinkles.

07 As soon as you have covered the whole cake in buttercream, take handfuls of rainbow sprinkles and press them onto the sides of the cake. I start at the bottom and gently swipe my hand up the cake to help them attach. Cover the sides and then the top.

08 Adorn your cake with a beautiful cake topper and watch the children's faces light up when you cut into the cake and they see what's inside!

DINO CAKE

Sink your teeth into this contemporary and vibrant choccy brownie cake.
So delicious it's terrifying. This is the ultimate cake for dino-fans.

Makes a 25cm (10in) cake

FOR THE CAKE

1 choccy brownie cake
(p. 80)

**FOR THE CHOCCY
BUTTERCREAM FILLING**

½ batch choccy
buttercream (p. 33)

**FOR THE BUTTERCREAM
FROSTING**

1½ batches buttercream
(p. 32)

orange food colouring gel

TO DECORATE

icing sugar or cornflour, for
dusting

115g turquoise-blue
sugarpaste

85g black sugarpaste

90g white sugarpaste

TiP:

I find using a metal side
scraper gives a nice clean
line. Just push down
firmly.

TOOLS

- non-stick mat
- silicone rolling pin
- metal side scraper
- sugarcraft knife
- ruler (optional)
- templates (p. 150)
- seven cocktail sticks

- 2cm circular sugarpaste cutter
- 5cm circular sugarpaste cutter
- paintbrush
- 25cm (10in) cake board
- turntable
- palette knife

Start with the sugarcraft work before baking the cakes or making the buttercream.
If possible, make the sugarcraft elements 24 hours before you need them, to allow
enough time for drying.

SUGARCRAFT

SPIKES

01   Dust the non-stick mat with a little icing sugar or cornflour. Using the silicone
rolling pin, roll out some of the turquoise-blue sugarpaste to about 6–7mm
in thickness. Aim for a piece that's about 16cm wide by 13cm high. Cut the
sugarpaste in a straight line along the bottom, using a metal side scraper
or a sugarcraft knife and ruler.

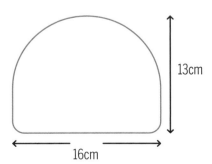

13cm

16cm

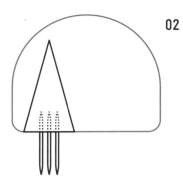

02 Place the large triangle template on top of the sugarpaste, lining it up on the straight bottom edge and to the left. Note its position. Remove, and place three cocktail sticks on top of the sugarpaste, evenly spaced along the triangle bottom. Ensure they are not too close to the bottom corners of the triangle or they will show when you cut it out. Press them in gently. Place the triangle template back on top to check.

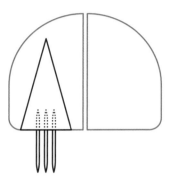

03 Now cut a line down the middle of the sugarpaste (to the right of the triangle template) using the metal side scraper.

04 Remove the template. Put the righthand sugarpaste piece on top of the left. Using the pad of your index finger, smooth all over to stick the two pieces together and conceal the tops of the cocktail sticks.

05 Place the template on top again and, using the metal side scraper, cut along the two sides. Set aside to allow it to firm up.

06 Using the small triangle template, repeat the process to make two smaller triangles. Use two cocktail sticks per triangle rather than three for these.

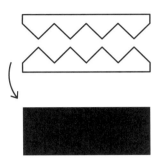

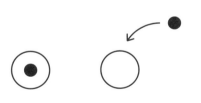

MOUTH AND EYES

01 Dust the non-stick mat with a little icing sugar or cornflour. Using the silicone rolling pin, roll out some of the black sugarpaste to about 4–5mm in thickness. Using the rectangular mouth template, cut out the sugarpaste mouth using the metal side scraper.

Take the 2cm circular sugarpaste cutter and cut two black pupils for the eyes.

02 Dust the non-stick mat with a little more icing sugar or cornflour, and roll out some of the white sugarpaste to about 4–5mm in thickness. Cut two white sugarpaste eyes using the 5cm circular sugarpaste cutter.

Roll out some more of the white sugarpaste. Using the teeth template, cut out two sets of teeth – for the top and bottom of the mouth. I like to use the metal side scraper for the long straight bottom and a sugarcraft knife for the triangular teeth.

03 Stick the white teeth on top of the black mouth. Using a paintbrush, brush a little water on the underside of the teeth to attach them.

04 Again, brush the underside of the black sugarpaste pupils with a little water on a paintbrush. Stick one pupil in the centre of each of the white sugarpaste eyes.

Once made, leave all the sugarpaste parts to dry on a non-stick mat dusted with a little icing sugar or cornflour. Do not cover, as they need exposure to the air to harden.

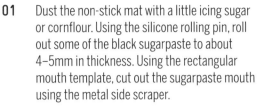

TIP:

If you don't want to have a chocolate buttercream filling, you can make two batches of the orange buttercream and use that instead.

MAKE THE CAKE

Prepare and bake the choccy brownie cake.

MAKE THE FILLING

Make the chocolate buttercream.

MAKE THE FROSTING

Make the buttercream and colour with the orange food colouring gel.

FILL AND COVER THE CAKE WITH BUTTERCREAM

Level your chocolate cake and place on the cake board. Fill with the choccy buttercream. Scrape away any excess buttercream, then cover the cake in a crumb coating of orange buttercream (p. 24). Now cover with a top layer of orange buttercream.

FINISH

Place the mouth on first, then position the eyes. Attach the largest triangle to the edge of the cake, central to the eyes, using the cocktail sticks to keep it in place.

Then place the two smaller triangles on the side of the cake, in line with the bigger top triangle.

You're done! ROARR!

TIP:

I use a side scraper to get a smooth finish, but I do leave it a little rougher than normal for a bit of texture.

ROARING ROCKET CAKE

Your mini astronauts will love this awesome rocket cake that's fantastically easy to decorate – a great introduction to cake making. Watch their eyes light up as it takes off!

Makes a large 23cm x 32cm (9in x 13in) cake

FOR THE CAKE

1 batch choccy brownie cake mix (p. 80)

FOR THE BUTTERCREAM FILLING AND FROSTING

2 batches buttercream (p. 32)

royal blue food colouring gel

TO DECORATE

2 ice cream cones
silver lustre spray
red jelly beans
strawberry cables
gold sprinkles
silver edible balls
yellow chocolate beans
chocolate stars
strawberry laces
sparklers (optional)

TOOLS

- 23cm x 32cm (9in x 13in) rectangular cake tin
- baking parchment
- pencil
- scissors
- serrated knife
- 30cm x 45cm (12in x 18in) black cake board
- templates (p. 150)
- offset spatula
- palette knife
- 6cm circular cookie cutter

MAKE THE CAKE

Preheat the oven to 150°C/300°F/gas 2. Line the cake tin. Make half the batch of choccy brownie cake mix. Pour into the lined tin and bake for 35–37 minutes. Repeat to make the second layer of the cake.

MAKE THE FROSTING

Make the buttercream and colour with royal blue food colouring gel.

SHAPE THE CAKE

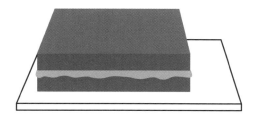

01 Level both chocolate cake layers using a serrated knife or cake-cutting wire and attach to the cake board. Attach the cake near to the top of the board to leave room for the ice cream cones at the bottom of the cake. Sandwich the layers together with blue buttercream. Put the cake in the fridge for 30–60 minutes to firm up, as this makes it easier to carve.

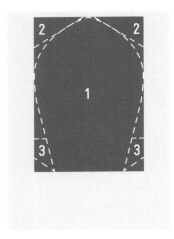

02 Using the template and a serrated knife, cut out the main rocket body shape. Use the offcuts to make the wings and attach them to the rocket with buttercream.

03 Use a circular cookie cutter to hollow out two small holes at the base of the rocket to insert the ice cream cones into later.

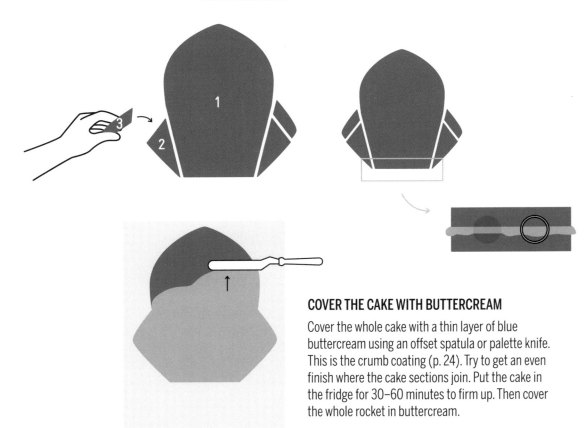

COVER THE CAKE WITH BUTTERCREAM

Cover the whole cake with a thin layer of blue buttercream using an offset spatula or palette knife. This is the crumb coating (p. 24). Try to get an even finish where the cake sections join. Put the cake in the fridge for 30–60 minutes to firm up. Then cover the whole rocket in buttercream.

FINISH

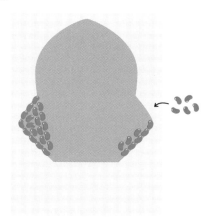

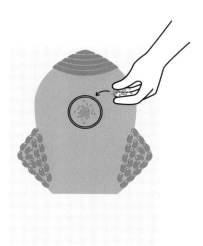

01   Coat the two ice cream cones in edible silver lustre spray. A few thin coats works best. Set aside to dry.

02   Take a couple of handfuls of red jelly beans and press them into the buttercream to cover the wings.

03   Cut strawberry cables to size with scissors and bend them into semicircular shapes to make the nose of the rocket.

04   Lightly place a 6cm circular cookie cutter near the top centre of the rocket cake to make a porthole. Fill with gold sprinkles and press them lightly into the buttercream to hold them in position. Gently remove the cutter and, one by one, press edible silver balls all around the circle to create a border.

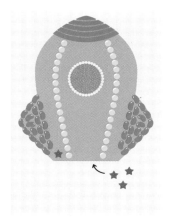

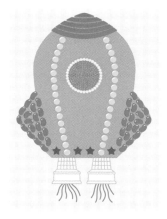

05   Arrange yellow chocolate beans from the top of the rocket to the bottom, curving the line slightly either side of the porthole. Gently press them into the buttercream.

Add a few chocolate stars along the bottom of the rocket.

06   Push the ice cream cones into the holes you cut out earlier. Use a little buttercream on the base of the cones to hold them in place.

Cut strawberry laces into short lengths and position them so they are coming out of the ice cream cones in a fiery effect. Add a cake sparkler to each ice cream cone for blast off.

5 . . . 4 . . . 3 . . . 2 . . . 1 . . . lift off!

5

BISCUITS

Biscuits are the perfect way to introduce children to baking – little ones love to get hands-on by rolling, cutting and decorating their own cookies. We have made thousands of biscuits at the BKD bakery, designing and hand-painting them for clients, and have a huge collection of cookie cutters in all different shapes and sizes.

Biscuits are one of my very favourite things to bake, and in this section I have shared the two basic recipes that I love best. They provide a zillion different flavour options, and always give a good smooth surface to decorate. Whatever flavour you choose, biscuits are brilliant and always go down a storm with children and adults!

SUGAR COOKIES

I love a fruity raspberry unicorn or a zesty lemon cookie. I use the chocolate cookie base for my messy minibeast classes.

Makes 12 large or
25 small cookies

INGREDIENTS

200g unsalted butter

200g caster sugar

flavouring of your choice

400g plain flour, sifted
(plus a little extra for
dusting)

1 medium free-range egg,
lightly beaten

TOOLS

- measuring spoons
- electric mixer
- mixing bowl
- sieve
- silicone spoon
- cling film
- baking parchment
- wooden rolling pin
- cookie cutters
- baking sheet
- wire rack

MIX

Cream the butter, sugar and flavouring together for 2–3 minutes until well combined. Start on a low speed and gradually increase. Don't overwork.

Using a silicone spoon, stir in the flour and egg. If using freeze-dried raspberry powder or cocoa, add it at this point.

Form the dough into a ball, knead lightly and then flatten it slightly into a patty shape. Wrap in cling film and chill for at least 1 hour. I like to make my dough and leave it in the fridge overnight: it gives the cookies a fuller flavour and nicer golden finish. It also breaks the baking up, meaning you can prepare the dough in advance and just grab it from the fridge when you fancy a baking session with the kids.

SHAPE

Preheat the oven to 180°C/350°F/gas 4.

Place a piece of baking parchment the size of your baking sheet on the work surface and sprinkle over a little plain flour.

Halve the dough and knead it briefly to soften it, and then roll it out to around 5mm thick. Sprinkle with more plain flour whilst rolling to prevent the dough from sticking to the rolling pin.

Take the cookie cutters and cut out the shapes. Push down firmly and give them a little wiggle to ensure they cut away cleanly. When you've cut all the cookies you can, lift away the excess dough. Leave the cookies on the baking parchment and transfer to the fridge for a minimum of 20 minutes. Chilling the cookies once cut prevents them from spreading in the oven.

TIP:

I find putting a chopping board under the baking parchment makes it easier to transfer to the fridge.

Cut another piece of baking parchment. Take the dough you've not used yet, give it a light knead and mix it with the leftover dough. Repeat the same steps of rolling out and cutting cookies until it's all gone.

BAKE

Once the cookies have chilled for 20 minutes, bake for 6–10 minutes or until golden. Bake cookies of roughly the same size together. Leave to cool a little, then transfer to a wire rack.

STORAGE

Cookies will keep for two to three weeks in an airtight container.

FLAVOUR OPTIONS

For vanilla cookies: Add 1–2 tsp vanilla essence or the seeds of one vanilla pod.

For chocolate cookies: Replace 50g flour with cocoa powder.

For orange cookies: Add 5 tsp finely grated orange zest.

For chocolate orange cookies: Replace 50g flour with cocoa powder and add 2 tsp orange essence or 5 tsp finely grated orange zest.

For raspberry cookies: Add 6 tsp freeze-dried raspberry powder.

For lemon cookies: Add 1–2 tsp lemon essence or 4 tsp finely grated lemon zest.

GINGERBREAD BISCUITS

A classic recipe perfect for gingerbread men or, another of my favourites, gingerbread dinosaurs. We also use this recipe at Halloween and Christmas, when the kids love to create their own gingerbread houses.

**Makes 12 large or
25 small biscuits**

INGREDIENTS

130g unsalted butter

100g soft light brown sugar

300g plain flour, sifted (plus a little extra for dusting)

3 tsp ground ginger

1 tsp ground cinnamon

1 tsp bicarbonate of soda

2 tbsp golden syrup

4 tsp water

TOOLS

- electric mixer
- mixing bowl
- measuring spoons
- sieve
- silicone spoon
- cling film
- baking parchment
- wooden rolling pin
- cookie cutters
- baking sheet
- wire rack

MIX

Cream the butter and sugar together for about 2–3 minutes until well combined. Start on a low speed and gradually increase. Don't overwork.

Using a silicone spoon, stir in the flour, ginger, cinnamon, bicarbonate of soda, golden syrup and water.

Form the dough into a ball, knead lightly and then flatten it slightly into a patty shape. Wrap in cling film and chill for at least 1 hour. If you're in a rush, split the dough into two patties and pop in the freezer for 30 minutes.

SHAPE

Preheat the oven to 180°C/350°F/gas 4.

Place a piece of baking parchment the size of your baking sheet on the work surface and sprinkle over a little plain flour.

Halve the dough and briefly knead to soften it, and then roll it out to around 5mm thick. Sprinkle with more plain flour whilst rolling to prevent the dough from sticking to the rolling pin.

Take the cookie cutters and cut out your shapes. Push down firmly and give them a little wiggle to ensure they cut away evenly. When you've cut all the cookies you can, lift away the excess dough. Leave the cookies on the baking parchment and transfer to the fridge for a minimum of 20 minutes. Chilling the cookies once cut prevents them from spreading in the oven.

Cut another piece of baking parchment. Take the dough you've not used yet, give it a light knead and mix it with the leftover dough. Repeat the same steps of rolling out and cutting cookies until it's all gone.

BAKE

Bake for 6–8 minutes, or until golden. Bake cookies of roughly the same size together. Leave to cool a little, then transfer to a wire rack.

STORAGE

Biscuits will keep for up to two weeks in an airtight container.

PIRATE SUGAR COOKIES

I like pairing up these cute little fellas with other pirate cookies: skulls and crossbones, letters to spell out 'ARRRRR' and delicious chocolate gold coins.

Makes 12 large or 24 small cookies

FOR THE COOKIES

1 batch vanilla sugar cookie dough (p. 110)

TO DECORATE

icing sugar or cornflour, for rolling out

35g skin-tone sugarpaste (per cookie) or food colouring gel added to extra white sugarpaste (ivory used here)

35g red sugarpaste (per cookie)

3g white sugarpaste (per cookie)

black icing writer or ½ batch royal icing (p. 38) coloured with black food colouring gel

edible candy eyes (optional)

chocolate strand sprinkles (optional)

FOR THE COINS

chocolate coins

edible gold lustre spray

TOOLS

- wooden rolling pin
- 7cm circular cookie cutter
- 4cm circular cookie cutter
- baking sheet
- baking parchment
- wire rack
- non-stick mat
- silicone rolling pin
- sugarcraft knife
- paintbrush
- medium circular plunger cutter (optional)
- piping bag (if using royal icing)

MAKE THE SUGAR COOKIES

Preheat your oven and roll out your vanilla sugar cookie dough. Use the 7cm circular cookie cutter to cut out the pirate faces and the 4cm circular cookie cutter for the gold coins.

Bake biscuits of the same size together, for 7–9 minutes or until golden.

CREATE THE PIRATE COOKIES

01　Dust the non-stick mat with a little icing sugar or cornflour. Roll out the skin-tone sugarpaste to about 4mm in thickness using the silicone rolling pin. Cut as many skin-tone faces as you need to cover your cookies. I like to cut out two at a time so the sugarpaste doesn't dry out and crack. Cut away the top quarter of each face shape.

02　Repeat step **01** with the red sugarpaste for the pirates' bandanas. This time, cut a quarter off the top of the circle and then a quarter off the bottom to make two pirate bandanas. You can reuse the centre piece.

03 Stick the two sugarpaste shapes to the top of the 7cm cookies using a little water on a paintbrush dabbed directly on to the biscuit. Secure by gently sweeping the pad of your index finger over the surface in circular motions. Where the two colours of sugarpaste meet, take the paintbrush and brush along the seam. With a sweeping motion, use your index finger to gently push the colours together. Continue until all your pirate cookies are covered.

04 Take a small amount of red sugarpaste. Roll one medium ball per pirate to make the tie area of the bandana. Flatten the ball between your index finger and thumb. Cut a triangle out of the bottom area.

05 Take the white sugarpaste. Roll six small balls per pirate for the spots on their bandanas, and then flatten between your thumb and index finger. You could also use a medium circular plunger cutter if you have one. Wet the backs of the spots with the paintbrush and press on to the bandanas. Take the red sugarpaste bandana ties you made earlier and attach these with the wet paintbrush.

06 Use the icing writer to add details to your pirates. Draw each one a mouth, eye and eyepatch. I also like to use edible candy eyes.

07 If you'd like to give your pirate cookies beards, use a little water on a paintbrush to dampen the area around the mouth of your pirate and make the sugarpaste sticky, then scatter with chocolate strand sprinkles.

TIP:

It's better to build up the gold in a few thin layers, rather than spraying one heavy layer.

CREATE THE GOLD COINS

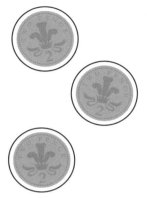

01 Unwrap the chocolate coins and place them on a non-stick mat or piece of baking parchment. Shake the can of edible gold lustre spray, then spray the coins from a few inches above. Allow to dry for a few minutes.

02 Take the 4cm sugar cookies and stick a gold coin to each one with a spot of icing writer or royal icing.

Ooh, arr! Yer finished, matey!

MINIBEAST SUGAR COOKIES

Spiders have never tasted so good! Not only do children absolutely love making these chocolate minibeast cookies, they also love learning fascinating facts: did you know there are over 25,000 different types of minibeasts in the UK alone?

Makes 12 large or 24 small cookies

FOR THE COOKIES
1 batch chocolate sugar cookie dough (p. 110)

FOR THE SPIDERS
(per cookie)
35g black sugarpaste

FOR THE BUTTERFLIES
(per cookie)
5g fuchsia-pink sugarpaste
25g lilac sugarpaste
5g jade-green sugarpaste

TO DECORATE
edible candy eyes

sprinkles

black, red and white icing writers

yellow mini chocolate beans

glitter icing writers (optional)

TOOLS
- wooden rolling pin
- spider cookie cutter
- butterfly cookie cutter
- baking sheet
- baking parchment
- wire rack
- non-stick mat
- silicone rolling pin
- paintbrush

MAKE THE SUGAR COOKIES

Preheat your oven and roll out your chocolate sugar cookie dough. Cut out the minibeast shapes using the cookie cutters.

Bake the biscuits for 7–9 minutes, depending on size. Bake biscuits of the same size together.

CREATE THE SPIDER COOKIES

01   Dust the non-stick mat with a little icing sugar or cornflour. Roll out the black sugarpaste to about 4mm in thickness, using the silicone rolling pin. Cut out as many black spiders as you need to cover your cookies. I like to do two or three at a time, so the sugarpaste doesn't dry out and crack.

02 Stick the sugarpaste shapes to the top of the
cookies using a little water on a paintbrush
dabbed directly on to the biscuit. Secure by
gently sweeping the pad of your index finger over
the surface in a circular motion. Continue until
all your spider cookies are covered.

03 Use the icing writers to add details to your
spiders – it also acts as glue. Use a white icing
writer in an oval shape for the mouth, then use
the red and black icing writers to add details
once it has dried. Add as many googly eyes as
you like, and sprinkles for a furry effect on the
legs. You get the idea!

CREATE THE BUTTERFLY COOKIES

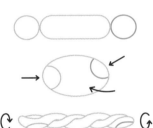

01 I like to use a tie-dye effect on the butterflies.
Take the fuchsia-pink, lilac and jade-green
sugarpaste. Push all of the pieces together
gently into a ball. Now twist the ball two or three
times until the colours blend a little, but are not
completely mixed.

02 Roll out, cut and stick on the butterflies' tie-dye
sugarpaste shapes using the same process as
steps **01** and **02** for the spider cookies.

03 I like to use a white icing writer to add details
to the wings, but you can use any colour icing
writer you like – glitter ones are pretty. You can
add lots of glitzy sprinkles to the wing area too.
I like using edible candy eyes. We've even seen
bright green butterflies with ten eyes at our
events. Get creative!

OREO™ EASTER CHICK POPS

I love making these no-bake treats with my family. They are quick and easy to make, and what could be cuter and yummier than an Oreo™ chick pop for your Easter celebrations?

Makes 14 pops

INGREDIENTS

icing sugar, for dusting

60g orange sugarpaste

154g-pack Oreo™ biscuits

1 bag yellow candy melts

yellow shimmer sprinkles (optional)

28 googly eyes or a black icing writer

TIP:

If you don't have a blossom plunger cutter, roll small balls of orange sugarpaste and flatten between your thumb and index finger.

TOOLS	
• non-stick mat	• heatproof bowl
• silicone rolling pin	• saucepan
• blossom plunger cutter (optional)	• spatula
• sharp knife	• 14 cake-pop sticks

CREATE THE CHICK POPS

01   Dust the non-stick mat with a little icing sugar or cornflour. Using the silicone rolling pin, roll out a small amount of orange sugarpaste to about 4mm in thickness. Cut four flowers per chick for the wings and feet using a blossom plunger cutter.

Roll 14 small balls of sugarpaste and pinch the tops to make a small cone-shaped beak for each chick.

02   Separate the two halves of your Oreos™ using a sharp knife. Roll the Oreo™ along the knife – that way there is less chance of it snapping.

TIP:

You can also melt the candy melts in a microwave, stirring every 20 seconds until completely melted. Add a little vegetable shortening if the candy melts feel too thick.

TIP:

If your kids just can't wait, you can put the Oreo™ pops in the freezer to speed up the setting of the chocolate.

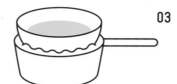

03 Set a heatproof bowl over a saucepan of simmering water over a medium heat (bain-marie). Add the candy melts to the bowl and stir for 2–5 minutes until melted.

04 Dip the ends of the cake-pop sticks into the melted chocolate and put them in the centre of each Oreo™. Carefully sandwich the two halves of the Oreos™ back together. Let the chocolate set for around 5 minutes.

05 Dunk your Oreo™ pops in the melted chocolate and top immediately with the shimmer sprinkles whilst the chocolate is still soft.

06 Add the googly eyes, wings, feet and beak. Set aside for 5–10 minutes to allow the chocolate to harden.

And eat!

CHRISTMAS GINGERBREAD HOUSE

It's beginning to look a lot like Christmas! This is my contemporary and vibrant take on more traditional gingerbread houses. I designed this template to be geometric in shape. It's super easy and perfect for little hands to construct.

Makes one house

FOR THE HOUSE

1½ batches gingerbread biscuit dough (p. 113)

one batch royal icing (p. 38)

TO DECORATE

sweets of your choice. I like:

coloured chocolate buttons

dew drops

fizzy strawberry laces

strawberry cables

mini marshmallows

heart-shaped sweets

edible silver or purple balls

chocolate sticks

desiccated coconut (optional)

icing sugar and edible glitter, for dusting (optional)

TOOLS

- piping bag
- writing nozzle no 2 or 3 (optional)
- wooden rolling pin
- templates (p. 150)
- pizza cutter or sharp knife
- baking sheet
- baking parchment or non-stick mat
- wire rack
- 23cm (10in) square cake board

MAKE THE GINGERBREAD DOUGH

Make the gingerbread dough and chill for at least 1 hour.

MAKE THE ROYAL ICING

Make the royal icing and put it in a piping bag. Cut a small hole at the bottom of the bag or use a writing nozzle in size 2 or 3. Set aside.

MAKE THE GINGERBREAD PIECES

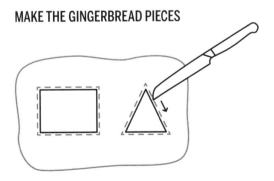

01   Preheat the oven to 180°C/350°F/gas 4. Briefly knead your dough to soften it. Roll out your dough to a thickness of 5–7mm, and use the templates and a pizza cutter or sharp knife to cut two rectangular sides and two triangles for the front and back of the house. Chill the pieces for 30–40 minutes to prevent them from spreading too much in the oven.

02 Bake the triangles for 9–10 minutes and the rectangles for 12–13 minutes, or until golden.

03 Remove the biscuits from the oven and leave to cool for a few minutes. Then put the templates on top of the biscuits and trim away the sides with the pizza cutter or sharp knife where any spreading has occurred. This will give you a nice clean finish. Leave to cool a little more, then transfer to a wire rack.

DECORATE THE GINGERBREAD PIECES

It's easiest to do the main decorating of the gingerbread house whilst you have all the pieces flat. Attach the sweets using spots of royal icing. I like to add chocolate beans in rainbow lines to the roof, and strawberry cables as a door with a silver edible-ball doorknob. I then build the house and add the rest of the sweets after that. Use your imagination here – the options are endless!

CREATE THE GINGERBREAD HOUSE

Once you have attached most of the decorations to your gingerbread house, you can put it together and add the finishing touches.

01 Take the two rectangular sides and lean them up against each other.

02 Pipe ample royal icing along the edges of the front triangle and secure to the inside edges of the two sides of the gingerbread house. Ensure you get all the edges lined up straight. Allow to set for a minute or two before attaching your back triangle in the same way.

TIP:

Remember to squeeze from the top of the piping bag.

TIP:

If you find you need some extra support, you can use a small tumbler between the two sides to hold them.

TIP:

You can use the same template to make a Halloween gingerbread house. Black, orange and purple sweets give a Halloween feel. You can add black food colouring gel to the royal icing to glue your house together, and also make great spooky cobwebs.

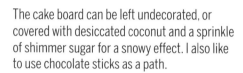

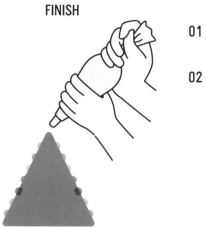

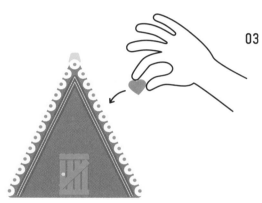

01 Pipe plenty of royal icing along the centre roof line and add decorations. I like to use dew drops.

02 Allow your house to firm up for 10–15 minutes. When it's feeling firmly set, carefully move the gingerbread house on to the cake board. Attach the house to the board with royal icing. Add more decorations along the seams of the gingerbread house to neaten things up. I like to use fizzy strawberry laces (cut in half length ways) and mini marshmallows, and then add silver or purple edible balls. You can also add royal icing icicles. Heart-shaped sweets make cute windows.

03 The cake board can be left undecorated, or covered with desiccated coconut and a sprinkle of shimmer sugar for a snowy effect. I also like to use chocolate sticks as a path.

You're done – ho, ho, ho! Merry Christmas!

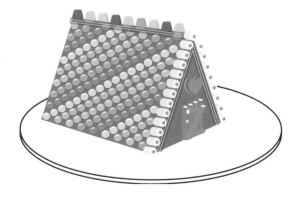

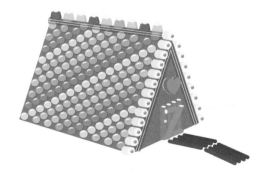

6

PARTIES

I love a theme, and creating my bakes around one. I get ideas from everything around me – fashion, product design, toys, travel, interiors, trips to the park . . . there's always something that inspires me. I've chosen some of my favourite party themes and styling tips, so you can make your child's birthday party super special. Delight them by creating a once upon a time fairytale party around my rainbow funfetti piñata cake, or why not take inspiration from my pirate cookies and let their inner pirate escape? My rocket cake with its sparkler boosters would provide an unforgettable grand finale for any outer-space birthday celebration.

ONCE UPON A TIME PARTY

A fairytale theme offers endless inspiration for magical party ideas.
Let your imagination run wild!

TIP:

Cardboard playhouses are perfect for parties. This cardboard castle not only entertains the kids, it also makes a beautiful backdrop. Adorn with glittery neon paper flowers for extra wow factor!

TIP:

My rainbow funfetti piñata cake works beautifully for a fairytale-inspired party. Top with a mystical unicorn cake topper and serve on pretty pastel plates.

TIP:

I love a bit of fancy dress – who doesn't? Invite the children to come dressed as princesses, knights, dragons or favourite creatures. Paper bag costumes are great fun.

TIP:

Fill the ceiling with lots of pretty confetti balloons, leaving the strings really long and curled. They'll soften the room and make your party look super stylish, and no child can resist balloons!

TIP:

For a fairytale feast, make a sugar syrup coloured with an electric-pink food colouring gel. Mix plain popcorn into the syrup. Sprinkle with a little edible silver glitter and silver star sprinkles.

PIRATE TREASURE PARTY

Ahoy there, me hearties! These swashbuckling party ideas will entertain children of all ages.

TIP:

Make a simple photo booth pirate ship using painted cardboard boxes and a few metres of striped fabric. The kids will love getting into character – complete with pirate outfits and inflatable cutlasses – for some fantastic pirate party shots.

TIP:

Fill a piñata treasure chest with plenty of chocolate coins, gems, rings and other goodies, such as pirate bubbles. Give the kids mini gold-handled boxes to fill and take away as party bags.

TIP:

My pirate cookies are perfect for a pirate-themed party. Put them in cellophane bags and use them to mark each child's place setting, or add them to your party bags.

TIP:

Spray Oreo™ biscuits with a few thin coats of edible gold lustre spray to make a yummy and super-simple pirate treat.

TIP:

Plan a party treasure hunt. Hide treasure in secret places and mark them on a homemade treasure map. X marks the spot!

TO THE MOON AND BACK PARTY

For a children's party that's truly out of this world, why not try these super space-inspired party ideas?

TIP:

Kids love to get creative! A giant cosmos poster to colour in together provides a brilliantly fun, calm and mess-free party activity.

TIP:

Rocket marshmallow rice-treats are an easy no-bake treat for the kids. Cut them with a rocket cookie cutter, and drizzle with white chocolate and sprinkles. Use a little chocolate to attach each one to the end of a cake-pop stick. Yum.

TIP:

Star sandwiches are great fun! Use a filling of your choice and cut the sandwiches with a star cookie cutter.

TIP:

Chocolates sprayed with edible silver lustre spray make fantastic moon rocks.

TIP:

Set the table with silver cups and plates, glow-in-the-dark straws and alien masks. I like using a black tablecloth with a glittery net over the top for an outer-space feel.

TIP:

My rocket cake is the perfect addition to this space-themed party and children will love it. Watch your mini astronauts' faces as it takes off!

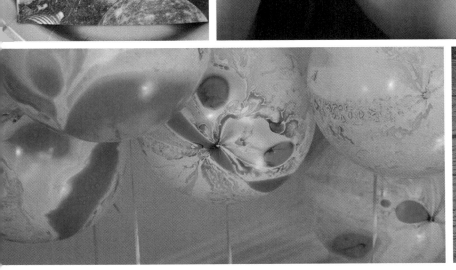

BITS AND BOBS

This section includes the templates required for some of the projects in the book. Simply photocopy or trace over the shapes with paper and a pencil then cut them out. Place the template on top of the sugarpaste or cake and use it as a guide to help you cut. You'll find most of the ingredients and equipment you need for my recipes and projects in your local supermarket or cake decorating shop, and there are lots of specialist websites to try. I've included details of a few trusted baking and decorating stockists and suppliers here, as well as some of my favourite ingredients and tips for where to source some fabulous packaging and party props.

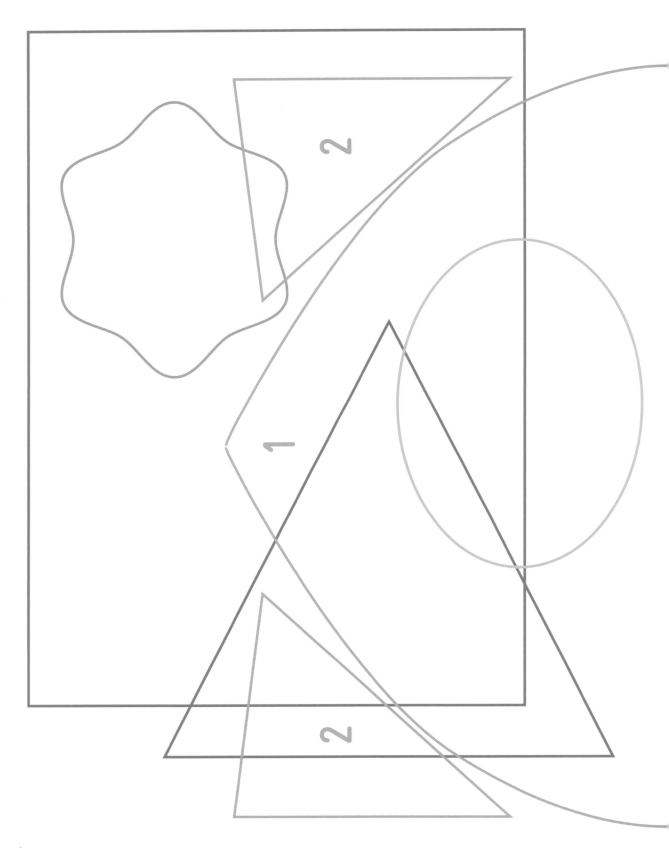

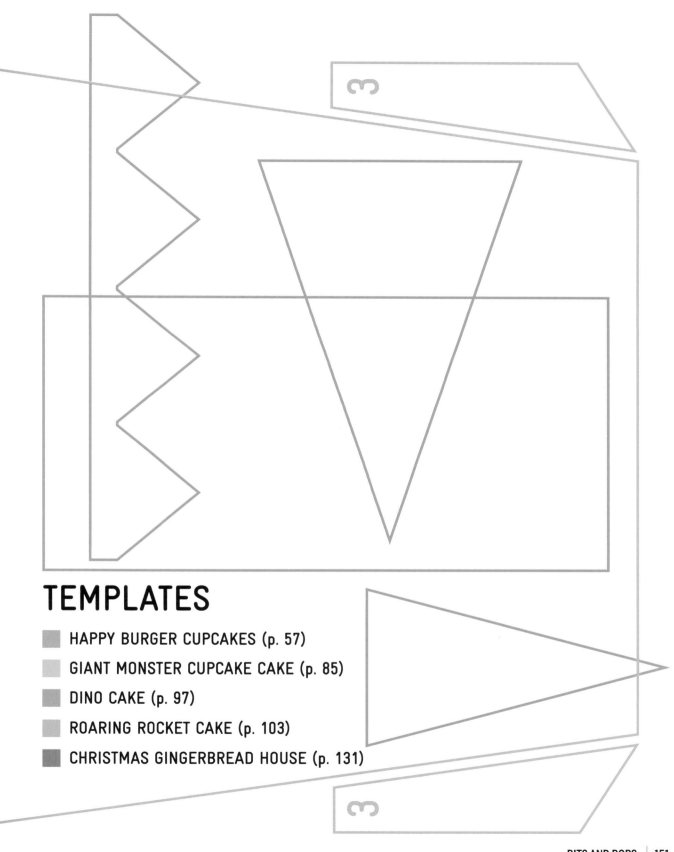

TEMPLATES

STOCKISTS AND SUPPLIERS

BAKING AND DECORATING SUPPLIES

UK

www.amazon.co.uk
www.bkd-london.com/shop
www.cake-stuff.com
www.craftcompany.co.uk
www.ebay.co.uk
www.hobbycraft.co.uk
www.lakeland.co.uk
www.thecakedecoratingcompany.co.uk

US

www.amazon.com
www.coolcupcakes.com
www.ebay.com
www.globalsugarart.com
www.wilton.com

Australia

www.bakingpleasures.com.au
www.cakesaroundtown.com.au
www.kitchenwaredirect.com.au

TOOLS AND EQUIPMENT

Giant cupcake tin
Eddingtons, available from stockists
listed here

Minibeast cookie cutters
Natural History Museum Garden Gang,
available from Amazon

Electric stand mixer
Kenwood kMix
www.kenwood.co.uk

INGREDIENTS

Flour
www.dovesfarm.co.uk

Butter
Lescure unsalted French butter,
available from Waitrose
www.waitrose.com

Eggs
www.thehappyegg.co.uk

FLAVOURINGS

Vanilla essence
www.nielsenmassey.co.uk

Natural flavourings
www.foodieflavours.com

FOR DECORATING

Candy melts
PME, available from stockists opposite

Edible candy eyes
Wilton, available from stockists opposite

Edible glitters
www.rainbowdust.co.uk

Sugarpaste
www.renshawbaking.com

Food colouring gel
www.sugarflair.com
and
Wilton, available from stockists opposite

Sprinkles
www.thecakedecoratingcompany.co.uk

PACKAGING AND PARTY SUPPLIES

Mini burger boxes
www.souschef.co.uk

Biscuit pop sticks and wrappers
www.yolli.com

Moon platter
www.lollipopdesigns.co.uk

Paper bag costumes and cosmos giant colouring poster
www.omy.fr/shop/en

Thank you also to some of my favourite suppliers who kindly supplied products and services for the photographs in this book:

AlexandAlexa (kids' clothes)
www.alexandalexa.com

Lola Beau (animal candlesticks)
www.lolabeaudesign.co.uk

Lauren Campbell (Adelle's clothing)
www.momxdad.com

The Kid Who (toys and beanbags)
www.thekidwho.eu

Little Lulubel (party supplies)
www.littlelulubel.com

Sarah Matthews (paper flowers)
www.sarahlouisematthews.com

Terri Pace (face painting)
www.facepaintfx.com

Lucie Pemberton (make-up)
www.luciepemberton.com

URIBE (Adelle's jewellery)
www.studiouribe.co.uk

ADELLE

Award-winning baker and entrepreneur Adelle Smith is mum to Cai and two stepchildren, Elsie and Stanley. She is the founder of BKD, a design-led bakery with a focus on children's baking events and kits.

Adelle's background is in design and market research, but when making her son his first birthday cake reignited her lifelong love of baking, she decided to turn her passion into a business. She launched her anti-kitsch children's baking classes from her home in Shoreditch, east London, and quickly started working with brands such as Nintendo, Toca Boca, Universal Studios and Fortnum & Mason, hosting private birthday parties and corporate events and making bespoke biscuits. Within a year, Adelle had moved BKD out of her home and set up a bakery. She then created a distinctive range of artisan, creative children's baking kits, now stocked by Harvey Nichols, Harrods, Fenwick and other major retailers.

Adelle's baking events and kits have appeared in a number of publications, including *The Times*, the *Guardian* and *Prima* magazine. She has presented at shows such as the BBC Good Food Show, and her video tutorials with Cai have been used by several brands, including Kenwood.

Only three months after launching BKD, Adelle found herself at the finals of the Virgin Foodpreneur competition meeting Richard Branson, and many accolades followed. In 2015, Adelle and BKD were awarded a Junior Design Award for Best Children's Food Brand, and a Loved by Parents Award for Best Activity Toy 6+.

Baked is Adelle's first book.

Adelle and the BKD team love seeing your creations! Please feel free to tag them #BKDBakes or get in touch through social media or at hello@bkd-london.com.

Follow us

- bkdlondon
- bkdlondon
- bkd_london
- bkdldn
- bkdlondon

THANK YOU

When I quit my day job, I could never have imagined the journey I would be embarking on. I have loved every second of writing this book, and have so many people to thank for helping me create something I can forever feel proud of.

Firstly, I'd like to thank my husband, Mark, who has been supportive of BKD from day one. You helped with the branding, listened to me go on and on about cakes, let me take over our kitchen and dining room in the early days, and picked up the slack at home whilst I worked around the clock. I'm so grateful for everything – love you lots.

Thank you to our kids, Cai, Elsie and Stanley, for inspiring me to launch BKD and for being so amazing, crazy and for making baking such fun. You're my little superstars!

Thank you to all my family: Mum, for your support when Cai was small and I was a one-woman show; Dad, for being a DIY expert extraordinaire and for making the stand at my first trade show look so professional; Natalie, Ashley, Paul, Ashleigh and Nanny Fowler, for acting as my sounding boards, testers and assistants. I feel very lucky to have such a supportive family.

Thank you to my BKD girl gang: Lisa Cobley, Charlotte Linzell and Lily Mindham-Walker. You guys make every day so much fun! Lisa, you have been with me almost from day one. Thank you for everything. I'm so grateful for all you do. Lovely Char-lotte, our queen of organisation, who started with us as an intern and couldn't bear to leave us – I'm so glad you didn't! Lily, thank you for your enthusiasm and for taking everything in your stride – you have been amazing. Thank you also to all the other wonderful BKD girls – Fiona, Livi, Parisa, Francesca, Esme and Aleena – who have helped make BKD a success.

Thank you to my agents, Vanessa Chapman and Jon Lazarus of Essential Lifestyle Media. I'm so excited to be working with you, and about what the future holds.

Thank you to photographer Dan Annett (www.danannett.co.uk). It's been a delight working with you on my first book. I'm so pleased with the result.

Thank you to designer and illustrator Cécile Dumetier (www.ceciledumetier.com) for being amazing and always going the extra mile. I'm so grateful to have you as part of the BKD team.

Thank you to Kate Burns, Sarah Finan, Miranda Baker, Paula Burgess, Megan Larkin and the rest of the Orchard publishing team. It's been such an exciting and rewarding experience working with you guys on my first book.

Thank you to the gorgeous BKD mini bakers – Cai Frejus, Elsie Smith, Henry Austin, Mollie Austin, Noah Clayton, Winne Dorrian, Thomas Linzell, Archibald McCurdie, Eugene McCurdie, Wolfe Poltock, Bess Thomas and Gabriel Thomas – who appear in this book. You were all amazing!

And last, but certainly not least, thank you to the kids who enjoy our events and baking kits, to the retailers that stock our products and, of course, to you, the lovely people that have bought my book.

Mwah!

INDEX